Finding

FINDING
A WAY

a Realist's Introduction to Self-Help Therapy

Alex Howard

Gateway Books, Bath

First published in 1985
by GATEWAY BOOKS
The Hollies, Wellow, Bath,
Avon, BA2 8QJ

Second printing 1988

Set in Palacio 11 on 12 by
Mathematical Composition Setters Ltd
of Salisbury, Wilts
Printed and bound in Great Britain
by Biddles, of Guildford, Surrey

British Library Cataloguing in Publication Data

Howard, Alex
  Finding a Way: a realists introduction to
                 self-help therapy
  1. Self-actualisation   2. Self-culture
  I. Title
  158'.1   BF637.54
  ISBN 0-946551-13-8

Contents

FOREWORD (*A CONFESSION*)

Much of what follows is commonsense

In other words ...

I regularly forget to put it into practice
And constantly need to remind myself about it.

One of my reasons for writing this book
is that I find that it is a way of telling myself
What I need to remember.

It has helped me

But my students are often better than I am
at translating the ideas into reality.

I have spent a great deal of energy
in learning to be good at *talking* about what follows.
This I find much easier, and more congenial,
than turning talk into action!

There is no reason why you, the reader,
should not travel much further than the signpost
that attempts to point the way.

1. Basic Attitudes

"If there is a God, He must be an under-achiever!" (Woody Allen)

Next time you go out from home look at the faces of the people you meet. How many have heavy, drawn fairly miserable expressions? How many look at you with suspicion? Do people seem as if they are getting a lot of enjoyment out of life? Do they smile? Do they look open and trusting? Or do they tend to shuffle along wearily, putting up with things and not expecting too much?

Well, there is joy and energy and enthusiasm to be seen, of course. But there are an awful lot of grey faces and heavy hearts. Do we have to be so miserable so much of the time? Look at your own face in the mirror. Is it glum and half-dead? Can you raise just a hint of a smile? Can you laugh at your serious, worried look? Can you laugh when your face is looking pleased with itself, or when it is self-preoccupied or pompous?

Most people will say that when they feel miserable it is because things *are* miserable; that they are 'right' to be miserable; that they have good reasons to feel glum; that they are *made* to feel sad by the sad world they live in. I want to question this. I do not want to suggest that we need never feel low, sad, depressed, or whatever other 'negative' emotion you sometimes feel; that certainly would be unrealistic. I do, though, want to show that much hysterical misery and common unhappiness is due to fundamental attitudes that many of us choose to adopt, that we don't have to adopt, and which are self-defeating. Such attitudes result in us feeling far more despairing and grey than is useful or necessary.

Does the World defeat you or do you defeat yourself?

I want to suggest a few examples of the ways in which we defeat ourselves. For instance: when we get up in the morning we may look at ourselves and (as it were) say to ourselves, "I'm still not yet up to scratch. I've got plans about how I should be and I am a long way from achieving these plans."

Then we look at other people and, again, quickly decide that, "other people are not yet as they should be either. There is a long way to go before other people behave as I want them to behave, think as I want them to think and feel as I want them to feel." Finally, we look at the world as a whole and, there too, we find that the world-as-it-is is woefully different from the world-as-we-would-like-it-to-be.

There is nothing foolish about having plans and wanting, and trying to make changes. That is an inevitable part of being human, or even of being alive at all as a human, animal or plant. Every living thing has needs and wishes it tries to meet. The self-defeating part is when humans say (as they often do) "I cannot be happy, feel fulfilled, get joy out of life until everything is more or less up to scratch, until things more or less fit my plans. Only then could I really enjoy life. Then my life could really start." If you take this attitude you are doomed to a lifetime of feeling that you are 'putting up with things' and making the best of a bad job, because if there is anything certain in this world it is the fact that we will all go to our graves on a planet that is still hugely different from the 'world-as-we-would-have-preferred-it-to-have-been'.

Problems or 'Probleming'?

Let us look at this from another angle. We start each day and perhaps for a very brief moment feel light and alive. Almost instantly the lightness goes as we remember all the problems that we have 'got to' face. Most people have a self-defeating attitude to problems. They tend to think that problems are a snag to living; that if only they could get all the problems out of the way then they could really start living to the full. Most people, essentially, tend to see problems as though they were rocks of different sizes. There are the big boulders that block your path through life. You have to get these out of the way before you can continue. Then there are the ones that get thrown at you. You suddenly get hit by a problem, or hit by a series of problems, as though you were the victim of an ambush. Then, finally, there are the big rocks/problems that you carry around with you, as it were, in a great big rucksack on your back. These make you feel heavy and slow your journey through life. You feel weighed down by them.

Many people take the attitude that problems are a damn nuisance that prevent them from really getting on with their lives as they would wish. They could really get on with the journey, they think, if they were not so often hit, and obstructed, and weighed down by problems from which they endlessly have to recover, get out of their way or get off their backs.

If the birds flying around outside could think as we do and could speak, then we would all laugh and see this craziness for what it is. Imagine a bird coming up and saying to you "You know I could really enjoy this life if it weren't for all the problems. The weather's turning cold, I have rheumatism in the wings, the neighbours are aggressive and don't altogether understand me, the nest has been damaged a bit, food is a constant problem, the children are always making demands and my spouse is not my ideal of a perfect bird! If I could only get all these problems out of the way and off my back then I could really live!" If such a thing were to happen then most of us would have the sense to see that all these so-called snags were an inevitable part of what it is to be a bird. That it is hard to imagine what a bird's life could possibly be without problems.

To put it another way, I think that it is useful to abandon the word 'problem' altogether. Instead of talking about 'having problems' it is wiser, perhaps, to talk instead about 'probleming'. Probleming is the very essence of being alive. It is the process of looking at oneself, other people and the world and deciding that you wish to make changes, large or small. Some changes are so small and easy to make, for example getting your socks on, that we don't call them problems at all. Others, inevitably, are much more difficult to achieve, and some are beyond our abilities and powers altogether. For example, putting your socks on if you suffer from a severe crippling disease. None of this need be seen as a snag to living, it is the very process of life itself. All of us, inevitably, because we are alive, are constantly creating a long line of changes that we want to make. We never get rid of the list because as soon as we have achieved those that are top priority we move everything up, and we constantly add to the list.

Sometimes people dream of getting rid of their list of changes to be made altogether, or of only having easy items to deal with. But on the few occasions where this happens it doesn't leave people free to 'really live their lives' because they then create a new item called 'being bored', or, 'not being challenged sufficiently', or, 'not having enough to do'. Having problems is hell, some of us believe, but the real hell would be to be without them. There is an old story which makes just this point, of a man who dies, wakes up and thinks he is in Heaven. Everything around him seems to be just as he would wish it. All his plans seem reality in this heaven all around him. As soon as he dreams up some new scheme as to how things should be, then immediately it is so. After a few weeks of effortlessly turning every blue-print that he ever had into reality and congratulating himself on having made it to Heaven, the man realises the deep ache inside him. There is no challenge, no testing of him, no risk of loss or failure or disappointment. The man realises that he was mistaken, that indeed he is in Hell.

What I am saying here is not essentially new. It has been said time and time again in different ways all over the world for thousands of years. But it seems that it has to be end-lessly repeated because, although deep down we know it to be true and recognise its truth, we continually allow ourselves to forget it. Much of the misery that is around us, I suggest, is the result of this forgetting.

This is not a rehearsal

This negative attitude to problems has all sorts of conse-quences and links up with other, equally self-defeating, attitudes. For example: Many people are not really putting themselves into their lives, heart and soul. They are holding back. Why? Because they are waiting for the time when, they hope, things are really going to get started. For the time when the world, and they themselves, are sufficiently 'O.K.' for them to justify being fully committed to it. It is as though they were saying, "I'm not going to put myself whole-heartedly into this world yet because it is not really good enough. I'm waiting for it to improve." Or, "I'm not going to get fully involved yet because *I'm* not good enough. I'll only make mistakes." Or, "I'm not really going to commit myself fully to these people because they are so much less than what I think they should be."

People can be on their death-beds and still be wondering if and when things are really going to happen. Or, more often, they decide that nothing too exciting or fulfilling will ever happen on this Earth. The best they believe they can do is hope that somehow they will be able really to live their lives after they have died. How? By going to Heaven as a reward for putting up with a grey, miserable world; follow-ing the rules and not making too much fuss. And so the ultimate craziness, enshrined in degenerate versions of Christianity and other religions; "I will really live my life, I will really get started, *after* I've died!"

Making a difference

How many of us would like to be all-powerful, to be able to do everything we wanted? Secretly, and not so secretly, I think, many of us would. When we are young some of us have great expectations about what huge changes we will make, what great achievements shall be ours, what an im-pressive mark we will leave on the world. We see wide horizons for ourselves, but then the world seems to close in. There are limits. Our strength, courage and ability are not what we thought they were. Our understanding is not as deep as we hoped. Circumstances are less kind to us than to others. What to do? If we are not Gods, shall we sulk? There seem to be quite a few people around who are sulking after they've discovered their limits and the world's constraints. "If I can't move mountains," they think, "then nothing worthwhile can be done at all. I shall simply pass the time; hang around at the edge of life."

It is easy to try to make changes when it is more or less

guaranteed that you will be successful. Great courage is often needed when you try to make a difference under tough circumstances; when you may very well fail! Most of us, (I include myself), are scared of risking failure, of making mistakes, of discovering our limits. And so we tend to take few risks and avoid pushing ourselves anywhere near our limits. We operate at a level of commitment way below our potential. We avoid making mistakes by avoiding making any real efforts. This, though, is the greatest mistake of all. The result is that we can easily tend to feel rather stale and unfulfilled, as though we were only firing on one cylinder, as it were. That, really, is all we are doing.

This kind of stuckness can feel safe and secure after a fashion. But it is the safety of being half-dead, of floating around in some stagnant pool at the edge of things while the stream of life flows by. The result of such holding back is the most self-defeating, self-destructive attitude of all; the view that "I don't make any difference to anything that really matters!" People think, "Even when I do make a difference to anything, it is in an area of life that is so small and trivial and insignificant that it is of really no importance at all." If you adopt this attitude you will always experience life as stale, flat and unprofitable; a pointless waste of time really, to be got through, somehow, with whatever distractions and minor amusements that can be found.

This basic attitude: "I don't make any difference", sometimes coupled with "nobody makes any difference" seems to be extremely common. The result is that people tend not to take themselves and their lives seriously. They are slipshod and careless about the things that they do at work, at home or wherever. They are just trying to get by.

Well, rather, let me not exaggerate. I am not saying that everyone is like this all the time, but that this does seem to be a very strong tendency in an awful lot of people. It is useless hanging around waiting for our lives to get started, *This is not a rehearsal*. This is not a practice-run for when things are really going to happen. Our lives already have started and for some of us life may be nearly over. This is the actual performance, and all that we can do, therefore, if we are to feel fulfilled, exhilarated, joyful, (as well as despairing), is to get going with our life right now. We need to stop holding back and saving ourselves in reserve. We need to get as clear as we can about what we want to do with our lives and try to use and develop whatever powers and qualities we may have to the full. In this way happiness will quietly appear (as an unsought-after by-product) and not when the world more or less fits our blue-prints. This latter sort of satisfaction is a relatively shallow affair compared with the genuine article, but it is often difficult to realise this because the pleasure of congenial circumstances is so much more immediately appealing than the fulfillment of discovering our own strengths and powers. We can never discover and realise our own potential if we always expect the world to fit our plans, which is not to say that I am advocating masochism or a callous indifference to other people's misfortune.

Chapter One. Basic Attitudes

Summary:

Fulfillment comes from unconditional commitment in world-as-it-is, not from expecting it to become the world-as-we-would-like-it-to-be. Problems or 'probleming'? This is not a rehearsal. We do make a difference. But no guarantee of success.

Questions:

1. Are you going to wait until everything is 'as it should be' before you find fulfillment in life? If so you will wait forever. Instead, can you see the sense in finding fulfillment in this world right now, even though you, other people and circumstances are a long way from how you would like them to be?

2. Do you see problems as a snag to living?

3. Do you see life as one long rehearsal for something that is coming in the future? When do you think the actual performance will begin?

4. Are you holding yourself 'in reserve' for when things are really going to get started? When will this happen?

5. Do you think you make any difference to anything that really matters?

6. Are you hiding at the edges of life in some stagnant pool? In what ways are you doing this? What do you fear might happen if you came out of hiding?

CHECKLIST OF SELF-DEFEATING ATTITUDES

Arising from Ignorance and Stupidity:

1. Problems are a great snag to living; if I could only get all my problems out of the way I could really live.

2. I am *made* to feel this way by circumstances and other people.

3. I am *right* to feel this way.

4. The present is really just a preparation for the future.

5. It is best to avoid anything that is 'unpleasant'.

6. I *have to* do most things that I do; I have no choice.

7. You have to manipulate people to get your way.

8. 'Happiness' is all about getting the good things and avoiding the bad things.

Arising from Insecurity and Low Self-Esteem:

9. My value as a person depends on what others think of me.

10. I don't deserve to be loved. It's good to feel bad. If people really knew me they would all back away from me in shock and horror.

11. You can't trust people, you have to be on your guard.

12. I cannot stand feeling confused, ignorant, uncertain.

13. Change leads to insecurity. You stay secure for as long as you keep the things you like fixed and unchanging.

14. I can't live without love. If my spouse (sweetheart, parent, child) doesn't love me, it means I'm worthless.

15. If someone disagrees with me, it means he doesn't like me.

16. I have got to keep proving to myself and others that I am a good person.

Arising from Despair:

17. I don't make any difference to anything that really matters.

18. Nobody makes any difference.

19. I cannot change the way I am. Nobody can change the way they are.

Arising from Perfectionism:

20. I should be kind, considerate, generous, dignified, courageous, unselfish — at all times.

21. I should be a really good friend, lover, parent, teacher, spouse, student — at all times.

22. I should be able to solve problems quickly and without fuss.

23. I should be able to cope with great stresses and tough circumstances without wobbling, cracking or showing signs of strain.

24. I should be a happy, serene, mature person who never gets swept away with childish ways, or fears, insecurities, conflicts, doubts and uncertainties.

25. I should be able to foresee what is going to happen, know what to do and understand what's going on — always!

26. I should be a spontaneous person but I should also control my feelings — always!

27. I shouldn't feel weak, ill, tired or sluggish.

28. If I am to be happy I must be successful; I must make really substantial progress.

29. If I am to be happy, other people have really got to improve the way they behave. The world has got to become a much better place.

30. If I am to be happy, injustice, exploitation, oppression, cruelty, inhumanity of all sorts, poverty, sadness of every variety has got to be eradicated. At least, *much more progress* has got to be made in all these respects if I am to be happy.

31. If I am to be happy, people have got to like me, agree with me, be fascinated by me. They have got to drop what they are doing and pay attention to me as soon as I appear on the scene.

32. If I am to be happy, I have got to get at least an average share of good luck. If I am very lucky that is good. But if I am unlucky then it is wrong, unfair and my happiness will be destroyed.

33. If I am to be really happy I need to become rich, famous and powerful. At the very least I need to be some sort of celebrity. I must have some sort of great success. My happiness will be in proportion to my success.

Arising from Avoidance
(which itself is the result of Perfectionism):

34. I can't get really involved in this world; it's just not (yet) good enough.

35. I can't really push myself yet; I'd only make mistakes.

36. I can't really commit myself to these people; they don't deserve it; they're not good enough.

37. Probably life will only get properly started after I have died.

38. I can't face myself as I really am. I can't face others as they really are. I can't face the world as it really is. It is all too painful. We must all just hide behind masks and distract ourselves with amusements as best we can.

This list is not complete. What other self-defeating attitudes can you think of? Which ones are particularly applicable to you?

Commonly, in my experience, people read this list and then add yet another self-defeating attitude:

39. I shouldn't have all these self-defeating attitudes.

This then becomes a new stick with which they beat themselves! More of all this later.

If you forget everything else in this chapter, try to remember this: "Men are disturbed not by things, but by the view they take of them". (*Epictetus, 1st Cent AD*)

2. Responsibility

Philosophers have discussed the subject of responsibility for thousands of years. The debate can get very deep and subtle and extremely complicated (also, sometimes, hopelessly sterile). In the next few pages I cannot hope to, and do not wish to, try to summarise what has been said. But no matter, because I think that as far as the ordinary layperson trying to make practical use of psychology is concerned, the subject of responsibility is much less complicated than is often made out.

It seems to me that many of us frequently don't take responsibility for what we do and also fail to understand what responsibility means. The problem, I think, is not that responsibility is so very difficult to understand but, rather, that we often don't *wish* to understand it. Why? Because once it is understood it is more difficult to avoid taking responsibility, and so there is a substantial pay-off in pretending to yourself that you are confused about the subject.

If I am responsible, am I to blame?

"Who is responsible for this?" says the angry teacher, or parent, or newspaper article, or government watch-dog. Often, the question really being asked is "Who is to blame?" or "Who can we make the scapegoat for this problem/crisis/disaster?" So that we can sit back, wash our hands of any responsibility, and pour venom, scorn and opprobrium of all sorts on the hapless victim who we hold to be the single and only cause of the trouble. Given these circumstances, it is hardly surprising that people try to avoid taking any responsibility. Surrounded by the irresponsible, they rightly fear that *all* the responsibility will be heaped upon them, and that others will refuse to face up to and admit the contributions that they have made.

The result of such bad habits is that we tend to think that if one person or group is responsible for something then other people and groups are not. This is almost always untrue. Responsibility for what happens is actually shared by a very large number of people. Each one of us has a contribution to make to what goes on around us to a far greater extent then most of us realise. This contribution is shared by many others, but that does not get *us* off the hook. Even with the very large events of history we each have a contribution to make. We are each responsible, even if we do nothing. Our doing nothing does not help us to evade our responsibility because the doing nothing then becomes our contribution! And a very significant contribution it can be. As Edmund Burke once said; "For Evil to triumph it is necessary only that good men do nothing." Some examples: A tyrannical dictator comes to power in the country. I DID NOTHING ABOUT IT — and so that is the way in which I am responsible. The world moves closer towards nuclear war. I watched the television at home — and that is my contribution towards it. There is widescale destruction, exploitation, starvation and this list can be much extended. If you did nothing, if you ignored these things, if you paid attention to something else, if you let fear and doubt get the better of you, if you didn't take the opportunities to find out, if you decided to do something else — then that is your contribution for which you are responsible.

Of course, this is not to say that you alone are responsible. Thousands and millions of others are, too, in their different ways. But one feature of the responsible person is that she or he pays attention to what her contribution was, and might have been, rather than bothering too much about what others could have done, or did and didn't do. Why? Because our own contribution or lack of it is the thing that we can actually change and do something about; and the responsible person is interested in making changes and not trying to justify inaction by accentuating the difficulties, limits and obstacles to change thrown up by other people and circumstances.

Really, you know, all this is fairly simple. If you are responsible you will tend to ask, "What can *I* do, what could *I* have done?" If you wish to avoid being responsible, you will tend to say "Look at all the difficulties, look at what others are doing wrong, look at how small I am and how big the world is". The responsible person tends to say, "If it's difficult and we are all fallible then I'll just have to try harder". The irresponsible person says, "It's so difficult, I feel so powerless, ignorant, fallible, that really there is nothing that I can do. I am not responsible. I give up".

Such is the excuse offered by the irresponsible person, but deep down he or she never feels very good about this. There is always a nagging unease. A feeling that really there ought to be more to it than this. That more ought to be possible. That the person is letting himself down. Well, there is more that we can do, we do often let ourselves down, but it is not easy to do more and it takes courage. We can, and do, go to great lengths to avoid taking courage in our hands. Let us consider one of the commonest ploys. A person avoids taking responsibility, pretends that there is nothing he can do, but deep down knows that something can and should be done about ... whatever it may be. He does not feel comfortable in his inaction. So, what does he do? He feels bad about it. He punishes himself. Feels guilty. Has a low opinion of himself. Tortures him or herself about it. And then eventually he feels better. People, as it were, say to themselves, "I've done nothing about this matter, but at least I've worn a hairshirt/sackcloth and ashes/whipped myself for days. And so I have paid a price. This *is* my contribution". And that is the contribution that people often make. They do nothing and then feel bad about it. Needless to say, this is not a useful contribution. It does neither themselves nor anyone else any good, only encouraging a pretence of usefulness.

Feeling guilty and feeling responsible are in fact quite separate matters, and yet when people say "I feel responsible for this", they often, actually, mean "I feel guilty about it because I feel responsible". In other words, feelings of guilt often follow closely on the heels of an awareness of responsibility. There is no reason why this should be, except that so many of us are in the habit of torturing ourselves about all the things that we 'should' be doing, and seeing ourseves as 'bad' people who should be constantly punished, criticised and condemned. Such habits lie very deep, and yet once we can see clearly that guilt and self-torture do nobody any good we can, very slowly and with determination, break the habit and abandon the foolish notion that it is good to feel bad about yourself.

Thus the responsible person is aware that she is in a position to make a difference all around her and that she is probably operating way below her full potential. She doesn't punish herself when she makes mistakes but simply tries to learn from them. Furthermore, she doesn't try to take action about everything for which she has some responsibility. Why? Because she realises that this is quite impossible. It is widely, but quite mistakenly, thought that if you are responsible for something you should do something about it, and that if you don't you are failing in some way. But we cannot possibly take action in all the options that are open to us. Life is short, we have to make priorities; to do one thing rather than another; and this means that the responsible person has to say "I could have done something about (whatever), but I decided to give other matters higher priority. I am responsible for doing nothing about this matter. I am not going to waste my time and energy feeling guilty about what I have done and not done even if I do later decide that I made a mistake about my priorities".

This is not to say that we will never feel regret or sadness about mistakes we have made. Obviously there will be times when we will feel deep regret, unless we are particularly callous and insensitive. But mistakes do not have to be sticks with which we can beat ourselves, and we do not have to endlessly imagine how things could have been and constantly lament, "if only . . .".

To repeat, then; I am responsible, but that does not get *you* off the hook. You are responsible, but I also have a contribution. And so we neither escape scot-free, nor do we need to collapse under the strain of thinking that it all depends on us alone. We pay most attention to what we can do rather than to what others might do, simply because we actually have control over one and not the other.

Free-will or determinism: A hoary old chestnut for philosophers

Is the environment responsible for what happens or am I responsible? The answer is, both, but there seems to be a good deal of confusion about this. Some people go to the one extreme of saying that it is all a matter of environment and heredity and that you are 'pushed around' by these outside forces. People to the left of centre in politics tend towards such a view. The boy is a delinquent because of his upbringing. There is nothing he can do about it. He is not responsible. The man or woman who is poor, unemployed or isolated is 'bound to' feel depressed, broken, violent or whatever. There is nothing they can do, they are not responsible.

On the political right there is a tendency towards the opposite view. Everyone is responsible for himself, the right wing politician tells us. Environment is not important, people must stand on their own two feet and take the consequences of their own actions without having others looking after them. Do-gooders, say those on the right, merely weaken people's own capacity to look after themselves.

Each side in this sterile political stalemate tends to see the truth in its own position without seeing the truth of the other. Both are only half-truths and each on its own leads to damage. To assume that a person is not responsible, or that she is less responsible than other more privileged people, is a great insult to a person, and if she too starts to believe that there is nothing she can do, she will become paralysed with apathy and stale hopelessness. However tough the circumstances there is always an enormous number of options open to people. It is always possible to get control over one's thoughts and feelings about one's circumstances. There are countless examples of people who have gone through the toughest conceivable trials and tribulations and discovered the truth of this. They have come out of very tough situations with a much greater awareness of their own strength, and discover this to be a source of inspiration, fulfillment and true freedom.

On the other hand, to assume that the environment does

not influence what people do is the opposite pole of nonsense and folly. Of course the environment imposes all sorts of constraints and difficulties for people. If I assume that because I am responsible then I can do anything and I am not limited in any way, I do not understand responsibility at all. I am simply suffering from delusions of grandeur! It is exhilarating to realise that there is far more that you can do about circumstances than you may have thought, but it is foolish fantasy to imagine that you can wish circumstances out of existence and act quite independently of them. An old saying, much quoted, and rightly so, deserves to be repeated:

> God grant me the courage to change what I can change
> The grace to accept what I cannot
> And the wisdom to know the difference.

There would seem to be a severe shortage of courage, grace and wisdom. For example, a government that merely thinks in terms of 'environmental engineering' and pays scant regard to personal responsibility can indeed take us towards the 'Nanny State'. Whereas a government that ignores the damaging effect that poverty and unemployment can have on people and refuses to accept any responsibility itself for these conditions is running away from its own obligations.

Changing the way we think and speak

A useful way of becoming more clear about the meaning of responsibility and, indeed, of acting more responsibly is to pay close attention to the way we think and talk. Certain language constructions tend to encourage an irresponsible view of the world, while others encourage responsibility. Let us look at some examples.

Changing 'have to' to 'choose to'

The more irresponsible we are the more we tend to think that we 'have to' do this and that. We have to go to work, have to follow the rules, have to obey those in authority, have to keep agreements we have made. And so, we pretend, there is no other option, we have no choice, we have to do what we may not want to do, we are not responsible.

The more responsible we are, the more we realise that there is, strictly speaking, very little that we have to do. There are usually other options. We could choose to abandon our work, to disobey the rules and ignore the authorities, to break our agreements. Even, to take a most extreme example, if someone holds a gun to your head and says "hand over your money", you don't have to hand it over. You can always risk taking the option of trying to dash the gun out of the person's hand, or arguing with him, or telling him to go ahead and shoot. Of course, many readers will laugh at this and decide that such alternative options are hardly viable because they are so unattractive. Most people would probably decide to hand over the money since this seemed the least bad option available, and I am pretty certain that that is what I would choose to do. The point, though, is that we do have a choice.

The responsible person knows that there are almost always other options and that therefore he is choosing what to do. This is not to say that the alternatives that we can think of will necessarily look very attractive to us. It may well often be the case that we like none of the options that we can think of, so that we are choosing the least bad without any particular relish for it. The responsible person knows that he remains responsible even when he is not attracted to any of the choices he can think of. Furthermore, he is responsible when he sees one option as the hot favourite and the others merely as non-starters. When one option seems an obvious choice then our choosing is easy, but it is quite untrue to say that this means that we really had no choice. Inevitably, there are times when two alternatives seem almost equally desirable (or undesirable) and then choosing seems difficult. At other times the moment of choice is so quick, easy and obvious that we fail to notice that we have in fact chosen at all.

The responsible person does tend to notice, however, and thus sees that she chooses to work, chooses to follow (most of) the rules and recognise (some of) the authorities. She chooses to keep to the agreements she has made.

"Ah", some will object, "sometimes this is not a choice at

all. Sometimes I don't choose to do what I really want to do. If I did what I wanted then all kinds of things would happen to me that I'm scared of. The family would complain, the police might lock me up, I might go hungry, everyone would be critical. All this makes me do what I really don't want to do." Obviously such circumstances influence the choices that a person makes; and people who have a lot of power over us, like being able to lock us up, or deprive us of our jobs or demolish our homes, will be able to influence the choices we make to a huge extent. Certainly it is true that a lot of our choices involve our choosing to avoid sticks rather than having a rich range of carrots to reject. Fear can play a large part in people's choosing. I avoid many options because I am scared of being rejected, of failing, of being attacked or because I am scared of discovering that I lack the necessary qualities for success. And I am responsible for this. I am responsible for letting my fear get the better of me. I don't have to do something because otherwise the consequences will be very tough. I choose to do something because otherwise the consequences will be very tough.

Changing 'can't' to 'won't'

Thinking in terms of 'can't' rather than 'won't' involves similar sorts of errors as in 'have to' versus 'choose to'. There are, clearly, some things that we can't do; if you think that there is nothing that you can't do then you are indeed suffering from delusions of grandeur. Try to walk through the wall or fly out of the window, and reality will remind you with a sickening crash that there are limits! But often we think in terms of 'can't' when really it is a question of 'won't'.

"I can't see you this evening, because John is coming," actually means, "I won't see you this evening because I have given John a higher priority on my time than you." (Whether this is through fear of the consequences or genuine attraction to the option is irrelevant as far as the fact of responsibility is concerned). Now, this is not to say that we should always go around saying 'won't'. It would probably lead to more fulfilling relationships if we were much more honest with others about our choices; but we might well avoid saying 'won't' if it was simply going to be taken as rudeness. We could find a way of being honest without being blunt, insensitive or indifferent.

"I can't come to the meeting, I have to see my mother" actually means "I won't come to the meeting, I have decided to see my mother", and so on and on with the countless thousands of examples that we can all think of in our own lives. It really is well worth looking at all the ways in which we avoid taking responsibility. It is not easy to change, but with determination and constant practice people can and do.

Changing 'need' to 'want'

Certainly there are some things that we need, although for bare survival these needs are minimal. More often we pretend that we need something when the truth is that we simply want it. People say 'need' instead of 'want' because they can then avoid taking responsibility for having these wants. "It is a need", they say, "and so I cannot be held responsible for it. For example, "I need to see John this evening", more accurately means, "I want to see John this evening".

Thinking actively instead of passively

The non-responsible person constantly sees herself as being a victim of the world; as being run-over by, or pushed around by, circumstances. The responsible person talks and thinks in a more active way, paying attention to what she did or didn't do rather than to what others did or failed to do. For example: "I *was held up by* the traffic jam", would be described by the more responsible person as, "I *know* that there are sometimes traffic jams and I *didn't allow* enough time to get here."

Being late is an interesting and important example. The more irresponsible we are the more we will tend to blame circumstances. The more responsible we are the more we will focus on what we could have done. When someone is really very strongly motivated to be somewhere at a certain time, they can reduce the chances of their being late to near vanishing-point. If I promise you a treasure-chest of good things, all for you, but please be here at ten o'clock sharp on Wednesday, you will be here! Only heart-attacks, civil war, plane crashes and the like are liable to stop you. Why? Because you will be so motivated to be on time that you will spend a great deal of time in carefully working out what possible obstacles there may be that could delay you, and you will allow yourself enormous time-margins to anticipate the most improbable hold-ups. This is why people are very rarely late for a job interview, for their holiday coach or plane, for their wedding or their mother's funeral. They are usually so strongly motivated that they give themselves large margins of error, and only the most improbable event will stop them being on time.

Now of course it would be absurd to give yourself huge time margins for every trivial arrangement you made. If a journey usually takes half an hour then most people would raise their eyebrows if someone regularly allowed themselves two hours for it. We would, rightly, say that the person had become obsessed about being on time. The truth is that we are usually very good at anticipating possible hold-ups and we usually know how likely they are to occur. People in towns know to what extent and how often the town centre is likely to get snarled up with traffic. The responsible person will assess all of this, consider how motivated he is and how much priority he wishes to give to being on time, and will then be prepared to accept that he will be late on a certain chosen percentage of occasions. The responsible person will say something like this: "I was late this morning, there was a lot of traffic in town and I am only prepared to allow forty-five minutes for this journey".

Such talk does not mean that the responsible person remains inflexible. If he becomes more motivated, or the circumstances change (gas mains being laid in town for example), then he will change his arrangements accordingly. It always remains under his control. The responsible person knows that circumstances influence the outcome but he never blames the circumstances. They are simply given and it is up to us to deal with them. Strictly speaking (and it would probably be useful to be more strict about the way we speak) the traffic jam does not hold us up any more than the buildings. If we said, "I'm late because I was held up by the buildings, they were in the way and I had to keep going around them", people would start to doubt our sanity. But the traffic jam is a 'given' just like the buildings. It is less regular in its appearance, but we are quite capable of anticipating it even though it is more difficult to do so.

An employer who understands all this will know that you are always responsible if you are late but his reaction will depend on the circumstances. If he is happy with the way you handled the circumstances then he will hold you responsible, (you *could* have done it differently), but not blameworthy, (you *should* have done differently). In other words, he will be happy with the time margins you have allowed and will accept that this will mean that occasionally you will be late.

Similarly, if a bank clerk hands somebody $10,000 of the bank's money the manager will hold the clerk responsible. Whether or not he holds him to be blameworthy will depend on the circumstances. Did the person merely ask for money as a favour, or did he threaten to shoot the bank clerk? If it was the former, the manager will probably decide to dismiss the clerk and take legal action against him. If the latter, perhaps he will thank him for not handing over more.

We tend to confuse blameworthiness with responsibility, but it would be in everyone's interests if we attempted to avoid this confusion. If you *can* do other than what you did then you are responsible. But you are only blameworthy if you *should* have done other than what you did. And, incidently, we are each responsible for judging what should and shouldn't be.

Being late, needless to say, is just one example. There are countless other ones that you can usefully think of where the same principles apply; where we think in terms of 'being held up by' or 'being done to by' circumstances, when we could more constructively and responsibly think in terms of our active planning, anticipating, making choices, arranging priorities and so on. *Doing* instead of being *done to*.

One more example of a passive (irresponsible) versus active (responsible) mode of thinking 'you make me feel ...' versus '*I* make me feel ... '. This is a critically important example and so deserves some time being spent on it.

Most people constantly accuse other people, or circumstances, of 'making'them feel angry, depressed, hurt or whatever and are therefore forever hoping and wishing that others would change and trying to get them to change. "If only other people behaved as I think they should", is the common cry, "and if only the world was as I think it should be, then I would be happy. But for as long as things are as they are then I have no choice but to feel depressed, miserable, angry, hurt (and so on). I am not responsible for being angry etc., circumstances are making me like this. Until the circumstances change then I cannot change." When you take this view of things then you have indeed made yourself a victim of the world, and your chances of finding fulfillment in it are very small. Failing to take responsibility for one's own feelings is one of the commonest forms of irresponsibility. Virtually everyone insists that they are not responsible for what they feel, and that it is others who 'make' them feel the way they do. Few people are prepared to admit that they have any choice in the way they feel; they imagine that feelings just 'come over' them like the weather.

I don't want to pretend that circumstances and other people are not influential in determining the way people feel. Clearly they are very influential indeed. If someone has had a life of chronic poverty, lack of opportunity, and has never had any real love or support from parents or anybody else, then no one is going to be surprised to find that the person *chooses* withdrawal and bitterness as a way of surviving, and has little trust in and concern for others. We will not be surprised at such an outcome and we will be much less willing to harshly judge such a person for his behaviour than we would in the case of someone who seemed to have been given much more love and material opportunity.

However tragic the circumstances, though, the real tragedy comes if a person decides "there is nothing I can do. I am made to feel this way by what has happened to me. I have no choice". A person is paralysed if he believes this, and it is never true. Thinking about this reminds me of an excellent television series that received great acclaim, "The Boys from the Blackstuff" by Alan Bleasdale (BBC2, 1982). In this series about life on the dole in Liverpool in 1982, Bleasdale explores this issue of despair with very great insight and sensitivity. We are shown a once proud working class culture that, as a result of chronic and widespread unemployment, is almost on its knees. Very large numbers of people are desperate and feel hopeless and, as we are shown the problems they face, it is not difficult to see how they have come to feel this way. Few of the T.V. audience, I think, would be foolish enough to pretend that they would necessarily handle things better if they were in the same situation.

Nonetheless, it is also clear that these feelings of despair, and the view that 'We are bound to feel like this', are doing these unemployed people even more harm than the material conditions of unemployment themselves.

A group of actual unemployed people in Liverpool was asked what they thought about the series. The response was that they considered it to be very true to life and that it helped them to realise that it was useless and self-destructive to give up. However tough things were, the series seemed to show, you could and should fight back, see how many options you could find and choose to avoid self-defeating emotions and thoughts, however understandable these may be.

There are always various options for action available, and it is inevitably possible to choose what you are going to think and feel about circumstances, even if your control over the circumstances themselves is very small. In other words, even at times of great suffering and oppression, (perhaps particularly at these times), it is possible (though not at all easy), to find reserves of strength inside yourself that you never knew you had, such that your struggle against the circumstances can take on epic and heroic proportions. You can even end up with a sense of achievement, and an awareness of yourself and your place in the world that go much deeper than anything you might have managed in easier times. This is not, of course, to justify oppression and misery simply because great things can sometimes come out of it. That certainly would be masochism.

Changing 'but' to 'and'

'I want this *but* there is that.' For example, 'I want to see some friends *but* there is all the washing up not yet done'. When people use the word 'but' in this way they tend to end up pretending to themselves that there are obstacles in, and conflicts generated by the world, when in fact the conflict is only within themselves. You get a much clearer understanding of your own responsibility for such conflict when you substitute 'and' for the word 'but'. Thus we get, "I want to see some friends *and* there is all the washing up not yet done". Or, better still, "I want to see some friends *and* I don't want to leave the washing up".

People use the word 'but' when there are difficult decisions to be made, and the trouble with this word is that it leads people to blaming the world and others for the difficulty of the decisions. Obviously the world has got something to do with the difficulty of making choices, in the sense that if the world were different the decision might be easier to make. This is true, but to blame circumstances is utterly self-defeating, because the world is what it is regardless of what you think about it.

All forms of gnashing against the world, however understandable, are self-defeating. The only fruitful activity is to accept every single facet of life as it just now is and then work out how we can best make a difference in it. The world is what is given. Within it, 'I want to see some friends and I don't want to leave the washing up' (for example). Instead of lamenting a world containing washing up, we can then pay attention to the conflict that is inside us – we want two contradictory things at the same time – and decide what we are going to do about it.

Conflicts inside ourselves are things we can do something about, these are therefore worth paying attention to. There is absolutely nothing we can do about the world as it is at this moment, and refusing to face this fact is a waste of energy. On the other hand, there is quite a lot that we can do about the world as it *might become* in the *future*!

The more a person is prepared to look into this question of responsibility, the more she becomes aware of the way in which many of the difficulties and conflicts that usually are thought to have been thrown at us by the world in fact arise from within us. Something is seen as difficult because part of us wants to achieve it, but another part is afraid of failure and rejection. (A third part, perhaps, might want to do something else altogether.) Take away the conflict within oneself and the previously 'difficult' task can be seen as a valuable challenge, or simply the next thing to be done. Or, alternatively, we might see something as an obstacle because we have particular expectations about how circumstances or people 'ought' to be. Take away the expectations about how things should be and what was previously seen as an 'obstacle' is now seen simply as that which is involved in doing what I want to do'.

Circumstances and people just 'are'. They only become 'a great opportunity', 'a damn nuisance', 'a terrible catastrophe', 'a wonderful piece of luck', 'a tremendous burden', 'a huge obstacle' or whatever, when we make *judgements* about these circumstances. The present circumstances come from outside us and are not under our control. On the other hand, all our judgements, thoughts and feelings about them come from inside us. They are our responsibility and they can come under our control in that we can make other judgements or no judgements at all. This is not to say that we should or shouldn't judge; that in itself would be a judgement. The point is that it is in our hands. Really understanding and acting on this is true freedom. It results in people not wasting their energies in trying to change what they cannot change, (ie. everything that 'is' at this present moment), so that they can focus their energies on what they might be able to change, (ie. whatever may be in the immediate or distant future).

Consider an example of how taking responsibility for our judgements, thoughts and feelings works out in practice. Let us take a really extreme example. Suppose someone has been tortured in a concentration camp and many of his closest friends and family killed. Suppose further that, following from this, the person feels angry, hurt, bitter, insecure, depressed, withdrawn from others and pessimistic about the future. Who could possibly be surprised if a person felt this way after such experiences? Who would judge these events as anything other than tragic and unjust? We are all likely to feel appalled to hear about such experiences and no one is likely to feel confident that they would cope very well if faced with the same stresses.

But consider what is happening. Someone has been tortured and friends have been killed. Nothing can now or ever be done to change this. He has suffered enormously, perhaps for years, with just thinking about all this. Again, nothing can be done about this. But what of the future? If he takes the view that "I am bound to go on feeling as I do; my feelings and judgements are the result of what has happened to me; there is nothing I can do", then he is indeed likely to face a future of un-ending misery and distress.

On the other hand, suppose the person says to himself, "I can get some control over the way I think and feel. I am responsible for these feelings. I am not benefiting from continuing to feel miserable, bitter and withdrawn. I cannot change the past but I can certainly change the way I feel about the future" – then there is surely a greater chance that he can change. Not that he will be likely to succeed at a stroke, that certainly would be over-optimistic. But change is possible. We know this to be true because there is plenty of evidence of people who have been able to rise above and learn from the most demanding of circumstances.

In order to succeed, it is necessary really to trust that change is possible. Courage and determination to change are also needed, plus an ability to see clearly just how and where present feelings and behaviour is self-defeating. Finally, it is necessary to be constantly kind to ourselves; to utterly accept what 'is', which includes accepting all our present self-defeating ways.

There is a great paradox in this. The more you accept yourself as you are right now (while keeping your determination to change), the more you learn about yourself and the easier it is to change. If I feel bitter and miserable right now, it *is* so. It has already happened and any regretting of this is a waste of energy. If you don't accept yourself utterly and completely as you are, then you simply waste energy trying to change what has already happened. If what you are doing just now seems to be a 'mistake' in that it is self-defeating or futile in some way then the useful thing to do is to see how and where it is a mistake and keep your resolution to learn from this and change. Getting tensed up about present mistakes tends not to work; it is just more of a distraction; more wasted energy.

Changing 'know' to 'imagine'

The irresponsible will often pretend that they absolutely *know* something to be true when the truth is that they merely have the *opinion* that it is so; that they think or imagine that it is so. Pretending that something absolutely is the case is convenient because we then don't have to take responsibility for it being our opinion. We can say "It is nothing to do with me; it just *is* so quite independently of me, and so I am not responsible". When, on the other hand, we accept that we may well be mistaken (and we often are), then we have to take responsibility for having the opinions and making the judgements that we do. Our actions then become the consequences of our judgements and assessments, and not something that we can put down to 'the way things just are'.

For example, a person may say, "I *know* the train will be late", "I *know* that we will fail", "I *know* that I cannot change", and then she can pretend that it has got nothing to do with her, and that she has no responsibility for it at all. A more responsible, and honest, account would be, "I *imagine* that the train will be late", (perhaps from undue pessimism or previous experience), "I *imagine* that we will fail", "I don't *imagine* that I can change"; and then the person has to face her responsibility for holding these views, regardless of whether they turn out to be accurate or not.

Pessimistic views about the future can often be turned into reality. If your expectations are very low you will probably, as a result of your own interia and lethargy, help to make sure that things turn out to be as grey as you predict. People often get what they expect. If they expect little they will probably get it. If they expect rather more they have a greater chance of achieving these greater expectations. This has limits, of course. At some stage too great expectations become delusions of grandeur. But we do, though, have a substantial influence on the outcome of our lives; to quote what I think is an old Chinese saying, "If you carry on in the direction you are going, you are likely to end up where you are heading!"

Changing 'it' to 'I'

"*It* feels good to be here" more accurately means "*I* feel good to be here".

"*It* is beautiful" means "*I* think this is beautiful".

"*It* is annoying" means "*I* feel anoyed".

"*It* is difficult" means "*I* am finding this difficult".

"*It* is a nuisance" means "*I* think this is a nuisance; *I* feel irritated".

"*It* is a disaster" means "*I* didn't want this" ...and so on.

We can all, no doubt, think of countless other examples. In the first instance, when talking of 'it' the person is not acknowledging his contribution and his responsibility. When talking of 'I', on the other hand, the person is clear about the differences between the circumstances of the world and his own judgements, feelings and thoughts about these circumstances for which he accepts responsibility.

The more you are prepared to take responsibility, the more you will talk of '*I* feel/think/want/judge'. The more you want to avoid responsibility the more you will talk and think in terms of 'it'. You will pretend that judgements, wishes, thoughts and feelings are not coming from you at all, but rather that you are *made* to feel this way, or even that 'goodness', 'beauty', 'annoyingness', 'difficulty' 'nuisance' and the rest actually exist as an objective entities in the world independently of you. It is sometimes accepted that "Beauty is in the eye of the beholder"; less often is it realised that every other judgement about the world comes from the beholder as well. I am not saying that, therefore, we shouldn't judge, but rather that it is of great value and importance for us to realise just where the judgements are coming from, and what are the (frequently damaging) consequences of these judgements.

Changing 'you' to 'I'

'*You* won't like this' often means '*I* don't like this, (and I hope that you won't either so that I am not the only one to have this opinion'.

'*You* won't be able to do that' often means '*I* don't think that I can do it and I don't want to feel that I am the only one who is getting left behind'.

The principle is very similar to that in the 'it' to 'I' examples. The responsible person is prepared to speak and act for herself, without worrying too much about whether others think along the same lines. The irresponsible person doesn't want to stand up and be counted for having his own thoughts, feelings, wishes and judgements, and so tends to conform with the crowd, or tries to pretend that others already think in the same way that he does. This leads to the very similar example of talking of 'we' when it is more honest to talk of 'I'...

Changing 'we' to 'I'

For example, *'We* are really bored' can often, more accurately, mean *'I* am really bored, (but I don't want to stand out as being the only one, and so I hope and pretend that you are all bored too)'.

Changing questions to statements

There are, naturally, many times when we are asking genuine questions, and these cannot be turned into statements. However, the irresponsible person sometimes asks what can be called 'pseudo-questions'. A pseudo-question is actually a statement disguised as a question. It is disguised in this way because the person does not wish to take responsibility for having made a statement; with all the attendant risks of finding that other people might disagree with, or disapprove of, the statement (especially if this involves a request). Let's look at some examples:

"Do you think it's cold here?" .. sometimes means, "I think it's cold in here, I want the fire to be switched on and I want you to guess what I want without my having to ask fot it". (In this way I can get what I want without having to take responsibility for giving my views and wishes).

Similarly, "Do you want to see my parents" sometimes means, "I want us to see my parents".

And, "Do you want to go out this evening?" sometimes means "I want us to go out this evening".

It is not difficult to tell whether or not someone is asking a genuine question. If it really is a question then the person will be happy with whatever answer you give. If it is a request or opinion wrapped up in a 'pseudo-question' then the person will probably feel irritated if you give the 'wrong' answer and feel angry with you for not having sensed that there was a request hidden away in the 'question'. The irresponsible person, using lots of pseudo-questions in this way, wants you constantly to be aware of what she thinks, feels and wants without her having to take responsibility for saying so and standing by her own views. This can be a very wearisome business if two people are both playing this game at the same time. Each wants to be rescued by the other without coming clean about what they want, and each is frightened of disagreement and liable to be very angry with the other for not being 'sensitive' and for being so 'selfish'.

Asking 'how' or 'what' instead of 'why'

If you tend to thrust responsibility for things onto others while avoiding your own responsibility, then it is not a good idea to try to explain your actions by asking 'why?', because you will simply hide behind defensive rationalisation. For example, if you ask yourself "why am I late?" you will tend to focus on circumstances and other people rather than on your own contribution. If you ask "why am I angry?" you will, again, pay attention to the actions of others rather than your own. We all of us, when things go wrong, tend to look at the ways in which other people and circumstances contributed to this, whereas when things go right we are happier to put the spot-light on our own responsibility. Success tends to be put down to our own efforts; failure is attributed to the dreadful obstacles and trying difficulties!

Take another example. If a quarreling couple asks "why did we argue?" you can be almost certain that they will each draw attention to the cruel things that the other did and said, and each will dramatically play down what she did. Each will pay little attention to the way in which he was perceived by the other.

When the question 'why?' is not working, when it is pro-

ducing irresponsible defensiveness, then a more construc-
tive question can often be 'how?' or 'what?'

"*What* did I do to be late?"

"*How* was I late?"

"*How* did I get angry?"

"*What* happened that led to us arguing?"

"*How* did we get to be arguing?"

People can still be irresponsible with 'how' and 'what'
questions, but it tends to be more difficult to get away with
it. 'How' and 'what' tend to help you attend to what actually
happened instead of to what you think should have happened, and these questions also help you to look at *all* that
happened; what others did, what the circumstances were
and, crucially, what *you* did as well!

Avoiding qualifying remarks

One common characteristic of people who habitually avoid
taking responsibility is that they will avoid making decisions
at all. After all, once you have actually made a decision it
becomes quite difficult to avoid taking responsibility for it.
And so the irresponsible person tends to be vague about
what he thinks, feels and wants. He hedges everything he
says with qualifying remarks, like 'perhaps', or 'might', or
'probably'. For example, "Perhaps I'll see you", "I might
come", "I'll probably do this".

The irresponsible person sees himself as just flotsam drifting in the river; or dead leaves blowing in the wind. He
doesn't believe that he can be categorical about anything
because, in his view, nothing is ever really in his hands. He
considers himself to be pushed around by circumstances that
cannot be predicted. Making arrangements with irresponsible people is extremely difficult because they simply will
not make a decision about what they will do, and they will
not stand by any decisions they do make.

A useful device, if you tend to be vague and evasive about
decisions, is to try to avoid making qualifying remarks
altogether, or, at least, try to keep them to a minimum.
Categorical statements like, "Yes I will ..." or "No I won't
..." or "I will if ..." can all help a person stop being
evasive. And if you really haven't made a decision yet you

can at least be categorical about this with a simple statement like, "I haven't decided yet". At least then, if you are constantly indecisive, you can take responsibility for this, and you can start to tell the difference between sensible caution and irresponsible procrastination.

"The buck stops here"

President Truman is known to have had a large sign with these words on his desk, addressed to himself and to anyone coming into the Presidential Office. People lower down in the hierarchy of authority in the U.S. government could always, when things got tough, 'pass the buck' to their superiors who, after all, were paid to take responsibility for the big and difficult decisions . A problem could be passed up and up the chain of command. Everyone could turn to his own boss and get him to take the difficult decision. But when the problem arrived on the President's desk there was nowhere else for it to go. No one else could be asked to take responsibility for the decision because, of course, the President was seen as the highest authority in the government. Advisers, consultants and specialists could be asked for their views and opinions and recommendations, but they were not responsible for making the decision. The responsibility for that was, and is, considered to be the President's.

Increasingly, we live in a world of large and growing organisations, where there is a strict line of authority and where the person at the top is nominally held to be responsible for everything that goes on in the organisation. This can, and does, go to absurd lengths. Many, and perhaps most, letters sent out from organisations are 'signed' by an authority-figure who has never seen the letter and who knows next-to-nothing, or nothing, about the matter being dealt with. For example, I regularly, in my work, get letters signed by the 'Director of Education' in a local authority, when it is perfectly obvious that the Director himself is quite ignorant of the relatively trivial matter involved, and quite rightly so. At the top or bottom of the letter, in small print, you get, "this matter is being dealt with by . . . " whichever person lower down in hierarchy it was who actually did the work and who knows all about it.

This particular sort of craziness is, I suggest, doing us all a lot of harm. It can inflate the ego of the person at the top to know that his name is attached to so many matters, and to feel that he is connected in some way with much of the action. It can help a person believe that his larger salary is justified when he reminds himself that his responsibility stretches so far in so many directions. But the person lower down the hierarchy is not encouraged to take responsibility for letters if he is not even allowed to sign them, and this sort of approach encourages illusions of power in the minds of the people at the top. After all, the authority figure cannot possibly keep abreast of all the minutiae in his organisation and it would be a poor use of his time for him to try. Why, then, pretend that his responsibility for the details is any larger than it is?

The top executive is indeed responsible for deciding on the main lines of the agenda of an organisation. She determines, if she is in authority, what the organisation should be doing in very general terms. But she cannot possibly be specific in all the details. These necessarily have to be dealt with by subordinates; and if the organisation is to work at all she must delegate to, and trust, those lower down the hierarchy. She must trust that subordinates will take responsibility for their particular work and deal with it as best they can; making their own decisions and *only in exceptional circumstances* referring upwards for advice or a decision.

This is the ideal way in which a hierarchy should work, although how far we need hierarchies at all is another matter. In practice, though, it often does not work this way. People make the mistake of thinking that because the person at the top has a general, overall responsibility then they themselves are not responsible; that they are simply ciphers who have to do this and that; that they don't really make any difference.

An organisation is doomed to ineffectiveness if it is full of people who don't feel that they make any difference and who don't own their responsibility. Most of the day-to-day dealings of organisations are in the hands of the great majority of people lower down in the hierarchy. The quality of the work will depend on the quality of the commitment of these (so-called) lowly people. If things are in a mess, it will be mainly due to the fact that so many people are not taking responsibility, not realising that they make a difference, and constantly asking others to make decisions which are more properly theirs.

There is a tendency to blame the system when we would do as well to also pay attention to our own, and other people's, irresponsibility. Of course, systems, mechanisms within and between organisations are important. When the system is a mess then the effectiveness of even the most committed individuals can be disastrously reduced. But we have become obsessed with systems and mechanisms, and imagine that nothing else is involved.

The hearts and minds and commitment of individuals are the most important considerations and we can often toy with mechanisms as a way of avoiding our own responsibility. However lowly a person may be in an an organisation, when he makes a commitment to what he is doing, when he takes responsibility, when his attitude of mind is positive and open, so that he actually wants to be of assistance to people – then his contribution can stand out above all others. He brightens other people's day, gives others new heart and energy, galvanises others into making renewed efforts. We all meet such people (more frequently than we realise), and they are often doing great things despite the most difficult and trying of circumstances, and despite the fact that their efforts are often unrecognised and unappreciated.

The person in authority who really understands all this doesn't shirk her overall responsibility, but neither does she try to take responsibility away from others. As much as possible she *gives power away* to others rather than *taking* it from them. If you think that you can only be powerful by *taking* power then you will not be very powerful at all. You will have under you an organisation of individuals who feel themselves to be powerless and who will therefore operate in a very slipshod and ineffective way, with little dignity and enthusiasm. If you endlessly give power away, on the other hand; constantly encouraging others to commit themselves to the full, to take responsibility as much as possible, to realise the difference they are making – then you will be part of a very powerful organisation indeed – one of committed, concerned, responsible individuals each offering all that they can and feeling fulfilled as a result.

The real leader, therefore, inspires and empowers. The effectiveness of her work may be difficult to detect because she is slow to claim credit and parade herself around. The ineffective leader, on the other hand, is full of a sense of his own self-importance, is constantly claiming credit for himself and refuses to encourage the independent activity of others. Everyone may know who he is, but little that is worthwhile gets done. This sort of leader is posturing. He is in the role of leadership, but he lacks the personal qualities that are required. A person in a position of leadership who does not have these necessary qualities to lead produces resentment, sullenness, hopelessness and ineffectiveness.

This is not to pretend that the system, the ground-rules determining the way an organisation works, the mechanisms, aren't also important in influencing effectiveness. Obviously they are. Moreover, the overall purpose of the organisation is of crucial influence too. If the organisation does not seem to be serving purposes that the people working in it can value, then the whole business will be anything but fulfilling. The challenge is to find a balance between attending to the mechanisms and their influence, and considering also the people involved and the contribution they make. The danger is that we can either consider the system as a way of avoiding looking at our own responsibility, or we can focus entirely on individual responsibility as a way of avoiding a consideration of the deficiencies of the system.

In one sense the buck finally stops only with the person at the top. But in another, equally significant, sense the buck stops with each of us, because we each of us have the last word on our actions. We can say. "I have to do this because this is the way the organisation works", or, "I think this because that is what the authorities think", or, "I believe this because that is what most people believe"; but ultimately it is we who decide to work according to the system, to follow the authorities and to believe what others believe. Someone can come down from the mountainside with tablets of stone and proclaim that they have the wisdom of the Ages. But it is for each of us to decide for ourselves; "Is this a reliable authority? Is this a true view?" and we are responsible because it is always open to us (though not necessarily easy) to think, feel and act differently.

We are responsible if we could have done otherwise, and

we are responsible far more frequently than we might think, because we could have done otherwise far more often than we might think. The more responsible we are, the more we are using whatever powers we may have to the full. However not everyone ends up with the same amount of power. Clearly, some people have far more power of one sort or another than others, which means that their responsibilities are all the greater. Everyone is responsible because everyone has alternative options. But not everyone has equal power and opportunity, and there are quite clearly enormous inequalities and great injustices here. However, we all have far more power potentially than we realise. A person who truly understands responsibility, and is really using his powers to the full, can and does make a substantial difference in this world; often more, indeed, than the weakling who happens to be in a powerful position in an organisation. In the latter case, the role but not the person has the power such that the person finds that he can achieve very little indeed and can do little more than hold the status quo intact. This is why it is that weak people in powerful positions can often feel as impotent about making changes as the people at the bottom of the hierarchy.

A final word on making choices

I have mentioned previously that the more irresponsible we are the more we tend to dislike making choices. There is the fear of failure and rejection and also the conflicts within oneself about what one actually wishes to do, that act as deterrents to choosing. There is a further reason why making choices often seems difficult. It is that, once you have made a choice, you have made a commitment to do one thing rather than another, to be in one place rather than another, to be with one person or some people rather than with others. In this way, the minute you have made a choice you have at least temporarily, and perhaps permanently, closed down other options. All the other things that you could be doing, and people you could have been with, are now no longer available to you.

To the extent that other people pay attention to this, they can feel that to choose is to lose. If you pay attention endlessly to what might be, to what you might become and to who you might meet, then you have little incentive to act and commit yourself at all. You prefer instead to go on surveying the vast vistas of possibility in front of you – or, rather, dream about them! Action of any sort reduces the possibilities, and so you remain a mass of potential rather than actuality; hanging around at the edge of life; looking at the whole of it from a distance without ever actually getting started at all.

Of course, few of us can manage to hold back from involvement to this extent. But a terrible amount of holding back does go on nonetheless. For example, two people can make some sort of commitment to each other, say in a marriage. They have made a choice, made a commitment, but a part of them holds back. Part of them, as it were, remains like an antenna sweeping around all about them, looking quietly for the 'Absolutely Right' person to whom they could 'really' be committed; looking for the 'fairy prince' or 'fairy princess'!

It is as though the person were saying, "I am living here, doing these things, being involved in these ways ... but just for the time being. I am partly committed, but I am still looking for the absolutely right place, the right person, the right things to be doing; and I am still waiting for me to behave in the absolutely right way. When all this is as it should be, then I will *really* decide and *really* get started, with no more holding back". There are satisfactions in dreaming away in our heads about the world as we would like it. To some extent the dreaming can help us bring changes in reality; but more often it becomes a way of hiding from the world as it is. We can get lost in our ideal world and pretend that we are 'really' there. With too much loss of contact with the real world we can pay the price of never finding the true fulfillment of commitment to this actual world; the only one that is available to us.

Chapter Two. Responsibility

Summary:

There is a pay-off in pretending we don't understand responsibility. Not the same as blame. 'Doing nothing' *is* a contribution. Others also responsible. The 'feeling bad' ploy. Responsibility not the same as guilt. Responsibility does not mean that we try to do something about everything. Grief and regret not the same as self-torture. Persons *and* the environment make a difference – it is not a question of *either* one *or* the other. Left and Right wing half-truths. We cannot always control circumstances but we can control our thoughts and feelings about circumstances. But not by repression. Responsible and non-responsible ways of talking and thinking. Acceptance of the world as it *is* – the enormous importance of this. Acceptance of ourselves as we *are*. Paradoxical fact that acceptance leads to change. Attitudes affect outcomes. Success due to our own efforts and failure due to circumstances? The buck stops with each of us. Decisions can lead to the closing of options – But decisions need to be made. Acceptance is not the same as fatalism, because you also accept that you want to, and can, make a difference.

Questions and Exercises:

1. What would be a more responsible way of talking and thinking in each of the following examples?

(a). "I have to stay in and finish this work this evening, and so I can't go out with you."

(b). "I need to clean up in the kitchen now; I am late with my work because I was held up in talking with John earlier on."

(c). "I did want to come out with you but there is all this work holding me up here that I have to do."

(d). "I know we'll have bad weather when you get your day off; but you make me angry anyway because you don't want to go out for the day whatever the weather is like, do you?"

(e). "It really makes me angry having to listen to you talking all this rubbish!"

(f). "It has been a really boring day! I have been driven into a rut by all the tedious chores I have to do everyday."

(g). "You wait until you see the new head of Department: you'll hate him. We are all tired of him already. He drives everyone mad."

(h). "Do you think it is a good idea to stay on late like this? Wouldn't you prefer to stop work now? What do you think about going for a drink this evening?"

(i). "Why did you talk to me in that angry tone of voice just now? Can't you see just what a big issue you've made out of this? You've made me very upset!"

(j). "Perhaps I'll see you at Judy's party next week. I might come but I'll probably have to fix the car first."

2. What is the difference between being held *responsible* and being *blamed*?

3. What is the difference between feeling *responsible* and feeling *guilty*?

3. Awareness

There is, I think, general agreement amongst psycho-therapists of whatever background that most people go around with a very low state of awareness, compared with their potential capability. It is as though most of us are half asleep to what is going on within and all around us; perhaps more accurately, we are at least ninety percent asleep. This may seem difficult to believe, because when you are barely conscious it is hard to imagine what it might be like to be more awake. It is only when you start to wake up (and this takes time, determination and practice), that you realise just how unaware you had been.

For those who are dubious about this I want to try to make the notion of our unawareness at least intellectually plausible. Why is it that we might be so dozy? Why are we so unconscious of things that we are perfectly capable of being concious of? There are several reasons. A very young child *is* highly aware of what is going on about her. She looks around her and within herself with tremendous attention, interest and enthusiasm. She has a very great energy for life and lives it with great gusto. There is so much about the world that she doesn't understand, but she is really keen to try to find out about it. She looks about her with awe, and with a very bright light of curiosity in her eyes. It all looks new and exciting and she throws herself into it and learns very fast.

As we get older, all this changes. Our views and our theories about the world become more and more firmly held, and increasingly shape our understanding of the world. To put it quite simply, we start to pay less attention to whatever is around and inside us because we think that we already know about it all. We don't look because we think we already know, and so, we think to ourselves, what is the point of looking?

This is not to say that we pretend to know all about everything; but, quite often, we don't look because we don't *want* to know or, similarly, we don't pay attention because we think that we/they or it *shouldn't* be like that! These are three of the major reasons for our staying unaware of so much that goes on, and they are each worth exploring in some detail.

"I don't need to look, because I already know"

It is a common complaint that the things we are familiar with, the places we regularly go to, the people we regularly meet, can begin to seem stale and grey to us over the years. We can even feel *ourselves* to be a stale and grey experience! "If only something new and different would happen!" we think, "...something unexpected and exciting that we could really get interested in and pay attention to." And so we constantly search for distraction and variety, for new stimulation, for change and movement.

Now, it is quite understandable that we want change and novelty; to see and learn new things. This is probably a motivation and need that is built-in from birth in all of us. What we frequently fail to realise, though, is that the world often seems dull and un-interesting not so much because we are genuinely short of variety and stimulation but because our awareness of it is so flat and lifeless! The spectacles with which we look at things are, as it were, foggy and grey, and so we can hardly be surprised to find that everything takes on a foggy and grey form. The world starts to seem dull because our awareness of it is so dulled, so that only the most exotic, or outrageous, or unusual, or hysterical, or violent, or dramatic can hold our attention at all. Anything that requires any sort of subtlety of perception and which doesn't jig about in front of us like some baby's rattle appears dull and flat to us. And hence our addiction to that greatest of all baby rattles – television – providing, as it does, new things to look at every two to six seconds. Hence also our addiction to The News with its conflict, pain, strong emotion, threats to society, scandal, and unusual behaviour; clearly journalists are in the business of entertainment and excitement on the cheap despite the pretence that we are primarily interested in information.

The more we become familiar with our surroundings the less we pay any attention to them. We think that we know all we need to know about what is around us, and we imagine that what we don't know isn't worth knowing. Consequently, we can go through the day and hardly notice anything at all. We travel to work without consciously seeing or hearing anything on the way. Our eyes and ears, let alone our sense of smell, are more or less shut down. Only the most unusual will catch our attention. Watch everyone as they travel on their regular journeys. They are often hardly aware of where they are going. Indeed, it is possible to walk or drive for miles without being aware that one has done it and without being able to remember anything about it. There seem to be no memories to recall because practically nothing was noticed and taken in the first place.

This is not true simply with regular journeys. It is equally true with the daily chores at home and at work. "We've done these things so often, we know about them so well that we need hardly notice anything about them or pay any attention to them at all. There is nothing new or interesting here." This is a common view, and so people sleep through what they are doing; functioning with extremely low levels of awareness.

Nor does the sleepiness stop with the chores and the regular journeys. It also continues with the relationships that people have. "I know my husband or wife so well", you think, "that there is simply no need to pay very much attention to what he/she is doing. And similarly with all my friends and the people at work and at the shops. I can predict almost exactly the sort of things that they will think and say and do. There might be the occasional surprise but there won't be many. I will be able to catch the odd, interesting and different thing that happens without having to pay too much attention."

This attitude of weariness, the view that things are essentially stale and familiar, shows itself in every aspect of life. For example, with body-awareness it is just as pronounced. People think to themselves, "I know 'me' perfectly well. I know how I will feel in different situations. I know the sorts of things I think and feel. I know what's going on in my body; after all, I've been with it, it has been a part of me long enough. I know what different foods taste like. I've eaten enough times, and so I don't need to pay much attention to any of this. I know what it's like to feel cold or hot or angry or elated or have a stomach-ache. None of these things need to have much attention paid to them."

The list goes on and on: of things we 'already know about' and so don't need to be very conscious or aware of. In the end, such an attitude can take over the whole of life. The youngster looks out with bright eyes; eager, curious and energetic. The older person looks out with a dull, bored, un-interested and lifeless face; as if to say, "I've seen it all before – there is nothing really new and interesting under the sun."

This can be, and is, a vicious circle. The less we pay atten-tion to things around us the more grey and un-interesting they seem to be; and the more dull things seem the less we feel the need to pay attention to them.

We think that we are very familiar with what is going on within us and around us, but the truth is that for most of us there are all kinds of obvious and important things that are staring us in the face that we do not notice at all. For exam-ple: People can go around for years with a tensed up jaw, hunched shoulders, or surly frown, or a jumpy manner, or an agitated pace, or a dead pelvis, or they avoid eye contact – and none of this is noticed at all! A therapist might say to a client, "Do you notice your tone of voice? You sound very apologetic to me" and the client for the first time realises that she has been behaving in this way for the past thirty years and has never noticed at all even though the behaviour is clear, on the surface, for all to see. Someone might have spent years with a lot of anger felt towards their spouse who might have been resenting it for just as many years. The anger might be obvious in terms of tone of voice, behaviour, posture and conversation; and yet it is not at all uncommon for both partners to remain extraordinarily unaware of what is going on. A group of people might have been working or socialising together for years. Each has got into a set role in relation to the others, there are patterns of interaction, regular recurrences of feeling and behaviour. But ask anyone in the group what goes on in that group and you will quite often find people have hardly paid any attention to what has been happening at all. They have been so wrapped up in their own immediate dreams or schemes or whatever, that they have scarcely noticed what they or others have been thinking, feeling, wanting or doing.

Most people, let me repeat, are scarcely awake. The common view is that there are just two states of living; either you are awake or you are asleep; and that you can tell which state some one is in by seeing whether or not he has got his eyes closed. I think it is much nearer the truth to say that there are degrees of wakefulness and that in some extreme cases people are scarcely more in touch with themselves and the world when their eyes are open than when they are closed.

Head Chatter

So what do we do to pass the time as we get on with the routine of living with minimal amounts of awareness and attention? Well, like everyone who spends a lot of time asleep, we pass much of the time in dreaming. The head chatters away almost endlessly with voices and visual images of how we would like things to be; how we will deal with things at some future time; how we would have dealt with things in the past. If there is nothing else, the mind will play tunes over and over again. We can spend so much time 'in our heads', as it were, with all this, that we are hardly in the actual world at all. We are not aware of what is going on around us and inside of us; we are not even aware of all this 'mental chatter' that is going on in our heads.

"But surely," you might object, "we can't pay attention to everything at once? We are bound to select what we will be aware of. We are bound to screen out things we are very familiar with or which don't interest us? And it is quite understandable if we push away things about ourselves and others that we don't like?" All this *is* true and understandable. The point, though, is not that we fail to be aware of everything at once and that our awareness fails because it is selective. Rather, our awareness fails because it hardly works at all. It is not that we fail to be aware of everything at once; that would be impossible; but rather that we are hardly aware of anything whatsoever.

What can be done about this? How can people wake themselves up? The answer is not by seeking ever louder music and stronger wine (not that I'm necessarily against these sometimes); a good starting place, rather, is to begin to realise that we are, indeed, nothing like as conscious as we usually imagine. Following on from this, we can begin to notice a little more clearly whatever it is that is in front of us or inside us that is now demanding attention. We can simply start to wake up to whatever it is that we have already selected for attention, and we sharpen our awareness of whatever this may be and simply trust that the process of selective attention will take care of itself.

Someone might say, "Well, that is no good to me because all I discover is a flat, dull feeling. Everything around looks lifeless and jaded. I feel dead and heavy inside". Very well. Start to pay attention to this deadness and heaviness. What does it feel like? Where is it? What is the shape of it? What muscles are involved? Where is the sense of heaviness?

You needn't try to do anything with any of this. Simply accept it, learn from it, watch it and go as deeply into it as you can. And then you discover a great paradox. The more you simply let what is just be, the more you find that it moves on to be replaced by new objects of attention, new moods and emotions, new body experiences. As you let all the objects of attention just be, the more they change and the more you understand what they are all trying to say to you.

This does not mean that you simply sit around doing nothing but merely watching. When the moment comes for doing things you find yourself doing them. There is so much that, as it were, takes care of itself. The more we watch what is going on within us and around us the more we realise that this is true. Not that we become infallible, of course. We trust that we can handle the next thing to be done and the next thing to be attended to. And we trust that we can learn from the many mistakes that we are bound to make; realising, in fact, that we can never learn without making quite a lot of mistakes!

'I think, therefore I exist'

We are all, I am sure, familiar with this chattering of activity
that goes on in our heads. It can consist of visual images, or
mental re-creations of sounds, or smells, tastes, textures or
body feelings. For most people it mainly involves visual
images, voices and tunes. The 'chatter' often seems like
various parts of yourself talking to yourself. Sometimes it
involves you imagining that you are saying to someone what
you would have liked to have said to them, or what you
want to say. The images can be of things you have seen in
the past, or of something you are expecting to see in the
future, or simply invented fantasy.

It would be quite interesting to try to make a film of what
a person's stream of consciousness is really like. There have
been a few films that have shown what is going on in some-
ones's head to some limited extent. But I have never seen
one that really shows the extent of the chaos, rates of movement of images, speed and tempo with which images and
sounds can move around.

Quite possibly you would get a headache if you tried to
watch such a film. Images would sometimes appear and
disappear so quickly that you would hardly have time to
notice them. In fact you might well miss some altogether.
One thought would lead to another and then another at such
a pace that it would be difficult for an observer to follow just
how it was that one image was reminding the person of the
next. And through all this there would be the vague blur of
the actual world outside, with just the occasional object,
person or activity being the mild focus of some brief and
sluggish attention.

What are we to make of all this? What is all this head
chatter for? Does it serve a useful purpose? How far does it
benefit us and how far does it handicap and cripple us? Obviously, quite a lot of thinking (to give it its more dignified
name), serves a very useful purpose indeed. We can
rehearse something that will or might happen in the future,
so that when the time comes we are more prepared than we
would have been. We can review something that has happened in the past, so that we can learn what mistakes we
made and resolve to avoid them in the future. We can

explore different, seemingly disconnected ideas and create a new pattern of understanding of them; actually create new insights and ideas. All this is of tremendous value to us, and it is a part of what distinguishes us from other animals with their smaller brains and consequent weaker creative and reasoning powers.

There are other benefits. When the pressures of the real world really do seem to be too much to bear, it can be very pleasant to drift off into that more agreeable world of fantasy that you can create in your head. And, in any case, this fantasy world can be the source from which we create new insights and goals and ideals for use in the actual world. If things seem a bit dull, and there is no music available, it is pleasant to be able to replay a tune in your head; although it is extraordinary the extent to which people can ignore the tunes they are playing in their heads as much as they ignore tunes playing on the radio. Finally, the idle drift of one idea leading, seemingly aimlessly, to another can pass the time of day and can also help you get clearer about various aspects of ideas and the way in which they relate to each other.

And so it is clear that a very great deal of the thinking that we do serves a very useful purpose, and it would be absurd for us to try to be without it. Insofar as the brain is like a computer (I don't want to explore similarities and differences here) then it is hardly surprising that a lot of time is spent in computing — processing the data you have.

So what of the snags? There are, I think, many. The chief one is that we can spend so much time being preoccupied with what is going on in our heads that we have little time left to pay attention to what is going on in the world and the rest of our body. In fact we are so preoccupied in our heads that we don't even notice that we are so absorbed. A person might be lost in some day-dream, for example, perhaps for ten minutes. He can then come out of that and drift on with some other string of thoughts; all the while failing to notice that any of this is going on and thus failing to see what it all means.

Obviously there are times when it is appropriate for us to think about what has happened or might happen; to play around with images in our heads. However, there are also times when it is more appropriate for us to watch what is happening in front of us. To listen, to smell, to taste, to touch, to be aware of what our body is doing, to notice where it is tense, how we are holding ourselves, to be aware of what we are feeling.

At such times the best thing our minds can do, if we are really to pay attention, is to SHUT UP! There are many times when we need to *stop* thinking; when we need to have a *still* mind, so that, for example, you watch without at the same time trying to reflect on what you are watching. You simply watch and *trust* that, if and when it is useful to think about what you are watching, you will be able to do this.

A person who can do this has great presence. Because he really is *present* to what is happening here and now. When a person with presence is watching a lake, or a person, or listening to music, or doing the washing up, then it is quite likely that that will be all that he is doing. At that moment it is all that he is. 'I am watching the lake' becomes, as it were, a definition of who the person is at that moment. All that there is for him at that moment is the lake.

People without such presence strike us as much more skittish and absent. They are never really doing one thing at a time, but constantly dissipating themselves with trying to do several things at once: watching something, thinking about it and several other things, searching around restlessly. Because they are doing too many things at once they are not really doing anything very well; there is not enough attention and concentration.

The restless, chattering mind really can and does spoil one's enjoyment of life. Suppose, for example, you are out walking in the countryside. To really appreciate this what do you need to do? If you really want to be in the countryside your attention needs to be given to the countryside and not remain in your head. In other words you need to *still* the mind and simply watch, and walk, and listen, and smell. This may seem obvious enough, but it is not what many people normally do for very long. They might manage to be by the riverside, say, for five seconds and then they will be saying or imagining to themselves, "Oh, what a lovely day. This is the best walk I've had for several months. It reminds me of the time we were on holiday last year. Some of the walks we had then were rather better, but this isn't too bad.

It's a pity we can't stay here longer. I wish we didn't have to go back so soon, I really don't want to be with the in-laws this evening. I'll need to get the potatoes on by six o'clock. That's attractive, the way the sun's reflecting off that water. It's a bit like that advert on the television . . . " and so on and on and on! A person's body might have been in the country-side for four hours, but they were aware of the place, attending to it, experiencing it, for maybe fifteen minutes! For the other three and three-quarter hours they were off everywhere else in their heads; looking around at last week, last month, six hours ahead, fantasising and so on.

It is the same with whatever example of awareness of body and of world that you care to think of. People might dream of what a good time they are going to have on holiday, they imagine themselves sitting on the beach and soaking up the sunshine. They bask in the image and enjoy these thoughts. The truth is that they are often paying more attention to the beach when thinking about it than when they are actually there. In the fantasy they are just on the beach, aware of it and with a still mind. But when the time comes for them to be actually on the beach their minds will not be still. They will be off again once more.

Often, you get more pleasure in anticipating what might happen or recalling what did happen than you do at the actual moment of the thing happening. This is rather sad, because the image is a very faint and feeble thing compared to the reality in front of you. There is the possibility of far greater ecstasy in really being here, now. But not if you keep trying to grab it with mental comments like, "this is wonderful, I must hang on to this!" because the minute you have done this you have taken yourself away from the moment of fulfillment, the awareness of the world outside, and replaced it with the dull comment "this is wonderful".

Why do we do this so much? Why do we feel the need to give ourselves a running commentary on everything and try to rush around in our heads in all directions at once, with minds jumping endlessly from one association to another? Such restless minds are not controlled minds. They are not being kept in their proper place and doing the useful work that they are capable of doing. Instead, they are generating a flood of images that prevent us from actually paying attention to the world we are actually in here and now. It is as though our minds were like a computer gone berserk; hurling data around inside itself with its control functions faulty and with its capacity to receive new inputs of data from the outside world seriously reduced. Why do we do this?

One of the reasons is that we think we *are* our minds. 'I think, therefore I exist' really does seem to be an assumption that we make for ourselves. And the consequence is that we can sometimes imagine that if we were to stop thinking we would disappear; that we wouldn't know where we were or who we were. It is as though a person were constantly pinching herself to make quite sure that she was really there. If you believed that you would cease to exist if you didn't constantly have the sensation of being pinched then you would always keep a firm hold of yourself! Of course, we all recognise that this would be a foolish thing to do, but it is hardly less foolish to imagine that you must keep chuntering away about everything in order to stay alive. Neither is chattering necessary in order to keep the mind in good trim or to understand and keep on top of everything. The mind can be of more use to us the more we can actually get control over it; the more we can prevent it from drifting off with random associations. Sometimes it is in our own best interests if we can shut up with mental activity altogether, and simply and quietly pay attention to what is going on around and inside us.

A major function of mental activity centres around labeling things. Labels are extremely useful in helping us to think about the world and to understand the way it works. They can also help us to focus our attention to particular parts of it. Thus a car mechanic with mental concepts like 'carburettor', 'spark plugs' etc. and theories about how an engine works, can focus his attention effectively to different parts of what in another's experience is merely a tangled heap of metal under a car bonnet. Having the labels 'carburettor' and so on really are of great help. However, with an uncontrolled mind these labels, and the whole process of conceptualising, can become a great nuisance in that they can actually prevent a person paying effective attention to what is in front of him. Instead, people can find themselves attending to the labels in their heads rather than to the things in the world that the labels are labels of.

For example: we can go around an art gallery and spend more time reading the titles and potted histories than we spend in just looking at the paintings. Or we can go around a garden reading the plant markers and thinking about how far each plant fits the general category, rather than actually looking at the plant. Or we drive around the countryside working out where we are in relation to everywhere else and looking at the map, rather than looking outside at what there is to see.

People will arrive at a new town and the first thing they want to know is "what is its name?" Giving names and descriptions to things provides us with a certain form of understanding. But understanding also comes from actually paying attention to things rather than simply theorising about them and labelling them. For people locked away inside their heads, this is often forgotten. Two strangers will meet. They wish to get to know each other. An important way of doing this is to pay attention to what the other person is doing; to watch and to listen. Another way is to hear the person's story; to ask for a set of categories; to put the person in a box. Quite often more can be learned by *not* doing the categorising and, instead, shutting up the mind and simply paying close attention to this person here and now in front of you.

To put all this very bluntly, it is undeniably true that learning and understanding can come from mental *activity*; that is, from conceptualising, thinking about things, categorising, reasoning, theorising about the relations between things, labeling things. However, it is also true that learning and understanding can come from mental *passivity*; keeping the mind quiet for a while so that you can simply look, listen, feel, without passing any comment or bringing in any mental images at all.

These two modes of being are in no way in opposition to one another. Ideally, they each support the other. Your active attention can be more effectively focussed if you have a great library of mental concepts available to you. Also, your mental activity can be more effective if you have been able to use your senses without constant interference from this mental activity. You can think more effectively about something if you have been able to watch it previously with 'peace of mind'. And you can watch something more effectively if you have previously done some relevant and penetrating thinking about it. The problem is that people in the West, in particular, have got a thinking process that is uncontrolled and which constantly interrupts them when they are trying to pay attention to something. Awareness of the world around us, and of ourselves within this world is thus considerably dimmed.

On the other hand, it is quite possible to go to the other extreme and make a fetish of body and sensory awareness at the expense of mental reflection. And so, for example, in the West we had the Hippie and certain Encounter Group sub-cultures that assumed that thinking was unnatural or neurotic, and that you could only really 'be' if you just went blank, 'felt the vibes' and stayed with here-now sensory and body awareness. To repeat, thought and awareness are not in opposition. They each support the other. Thus, it is a poor thinker who cannot ever pay attention, and it is an insensitive person who cannot ever reflect on what he has been attending to.

All too often such damaging divisions are made. A similar one is the split suggested between thought, feeling and action. People tend to see themselves as either 'the thinking sort', or 'sensitive, emotional types', or 'men of action' ... as though you had to make a choice. Each mode of being ideally supports the other two and is supported by them. None of them is strictly separable from the others; (thus, for example, what you *feel* is usually influenced by what you *think*, as in "I *feel* angry because I *think* that she should have behaved differently") *Feeling* divorced from adequate *thought* is often infantile, *thought* without *feeling* is arid and inhuman, *thought* without *action* is irrelevant and academic (as in 'makes no difference') *action* without *thought* is ill-informed — and so on. So often, when the balance is set too far towards one mode of being, it creates a reaction to some other extreme, so that polarisation of view and division takes place. For example, many have become critical of the misuse of intellect and the way it can lead to people 'living in their heads' without awareness, and also to defensive rationalisation and a withdrawal from responsible involvement in the world. The intellectual, if he misuses intellect, can use it as a way of avoiding any action and participation in the world; he can become a voyeur. But, sadly, this can and has led to, a reaction to the other extreme where people become positively anti-intellectual, opposed to thinking, and make a fetish instead of awareness of (simple) things around them and of their own feelings within them. People then start to talk about 'going beyond mind', but, sadly, they try to do this before they have developed a mind to go beyond and before they have worked out what this 'going beyond' could possibly mean.

The obsession with the future

The great advantage of our mind is that it can bring to our attention aspects of the world that are not immediately in front of us and try to sort out how we are going to deal with these aspects on some future occasion when they might be there before us. In other words, we can rehearse how we will act and perceive things tomorrow, or next week, or next year. The very notion of time arises precisely from this ability to conjure up images of things that are not in front of us. We have mental images of what was, and thus we form the concept of the past. We have mental images of what might be or will be and thus we form a concept of the future. If all that we could do was to attend to here and now and if we never reflected on any of this, then there would only be here and now for us. With only an awareness of here and now, and no thought about past and future, time would, as it were, disappear for us. We would not even have a concept of the present because this concept only exists in relation to the concepts of past and future.

Eternity means being outside of time, rather than 'a very long time'. When we pay full attention to things that are happening here and now, and act here and now, then we 'lose track of time', lose our preoccupation with time altogether. Action and awareness are in one sense outside of time; it is the *thinking* about actions and awareness that brings in time. You can imagine yourself to be a slave of time, pushed around by and limited by it, as soon as you start thinking and making plans. You are quite independent of time for as long as you are simply doing and watching here and now, because when you are doing this that is all that there is. I say this not in order to suggest that we should stop thinking so as to escape from the ravages of time, but in order to show that the so-called 'pressure of time' is in fact the pressure of *ourselves* making demands upon, and plans for, ourselves.

Because our mental activity is so dominant, and our ability to be quietly aware so stunted, we tend to see time as terribly important and the future as much more important than the present. The mind is most interested in the future because it is designed to help us prepare for it . Because we think that we *are* our minds, we tend to think that the whole purpose of life is to prepare for the future. And so we tend to ask "What am I living *for*?" as though the whole of life were a preparation for some great final outcome that will give meaning and sense to all that happened previously. It is as though we were all waiting for the final punch-line that will explain everything that came before. With mental activity we rehearse and rehearse; we think that mental activity is who we are and so we think that life is just one big rehearsal. And thus we ask "What is it all a rehearsal *for*? What are we living *for*?"

On those occasions when we don't lose ourselves in mental activity, and instead remain aware of now and of what we are doing now, then the question "what are you living *for*?" simply disappears. The question can then become, "What ... are you *living*?" And the answer is clear to us. We are alive when we are awake, when we are aware. The more aware we are, the more alive we are. Also, it becomes obvious that the only time that we can be alive at all is here and now. Life then stops being a mental rehearsal for something else; it consists instead of committed action and awareness here, and now. The point of life becomes to live it. Mental activity takes its proper place as just one form of action and doesn't dominate us. It becomes something that we sometimes do here and now and that we are aware of doing. We do not get lost within it and we do not let it take over the whole of life at the expense of other activity and the awareness of everything else that is going on within and around us.

When we are lost in our minds, we tend to see life as a problem to be solved. When we live with awareness we tend to see life as a mystery to be lived.

The person lost in his mind tends to see life as a journey with the whole point of it being to arrive at the 'right' place, whatever or wherever that might be. But when we are not lost in our minds but are instead alive and doing here and now, then we see life as a journey where any arrival is a complete mystery but where the point of it is to live it, to be on the journey, savouring it to the full.

We see then that if life is like a journey it is not like the journey of a commuter, who is anxious to be at the right place at the right time and who sees the actual travelling as a chore and an obstacle. Instead, it is like the journey involved in an adventure; where we are moving forward to nobody knows where for sure; where we can only ever scout ahead of us to some limited extent; but where the point of it all is to learn all we can about who we are and what there is to see all around us, and find fulfillment in each moment as it comes. We can then trust that we will choose and deal with the next thing to be done as best we can, and learn from whatever mistakes we make.

When we are lost in thought, the point of life seems to be to get clear about the destination and to be fully prepared for it. With awareness, thinking simply becomes a potentially useful part of living, and the point of life is seen to be to live it and to trust that this can be done. This does not mean that thinking is abandoned. It can be very useful in helping us to map our way ahead a little. But it always remains clear that thinking can never be the whole of life. It can only map the way ahead to a limited extent and it can never effectively replace awareness and non-mental activity. Thinking can help us prepare, but fulfillment can only come from awareness of ourselves and our world and actual behavour in it. If all that we do is to think, then we lose awareness, even of the fact that we are thinking, and we never participate. Then even our mental rehearsal becomes pointless, because we never actually do anything with the thought.

This phenomenon of not really participating in life can be quite common in those who place too much store by mental rehearsal. If we take the view that we must form the best possible picture of what is to be done, with a clear view of

all the snags and alternatives, before we actually get down
to do anything, then we will end up not doing anything at
all. Mental preparation can always be extended and can
never be completed, and so if we wait for us to complete it
we will never actually take part in life at all. Moreover,
because we are not taking part and thus learning from our
mistakes, the quality of our mental learning will in any case
be severely diminished. In this way, people can paralyze
themselves. Action is prevented by the constant interference
of mental rehearsal. It is as though the person was trying to
get a complete and final hold on life through mental activity.
People try and try to do this but it simply cannot be done.
With mental activity we try to 'know' the way that is ahead
of us. The less we feel safe in the world the more we try to
get a certain picture of what is coming next, through more
and more feverish mental activity. But the truth is that we
can never get a certain, final, picture. We simply have to let
go and trust. And we have to trust that we can discover
when it is time to abandon mental rehearsal and get on with
something else.

Avoiding awareness of feelings

"I don't know because I don't *want* to know"
"I don't know because it *shouldn't* be like this"
When people feel 'good', they are usually quick to be aware
of it and they like to hang on to such good feelings for as
long as possible. As we have seen, though, this very process
of trying to hang on to the feeling itself gets rid of it, because
you have then replaced the 'good' feeling with the 'less
good' feelings of anxiety, insecurity, desperation, tensed-up
clinging, fear of what the future might bring, and so on.

On the other hand, when people feel 'bad', they usually
do not wish to have such feelings and they resist experiencing them. People try to avoid being aware of bad feelings;
they push them away, and often succeed in remaining unconscious of them. If you feel bad but you are not aware of
this, it doesn't mean to say that you have got rid of the feeling. To get rid of the awareness of a feeling is not to get rid
of the feeling itself. And so it is that people have all sorts of
(so-called) bad feelings, like fear, confusion, anxiety, internal

conflict, insecurity, anger, despair, hatred, resentment, disillusionment, that they are not aware of. I am not saying that we successfully keep from awareness all these feelings all the time, but that we are quite good at keeping a large proportion of them beneath the level of conscious awareness.

This means, of course, that we remain unaware not only of the feelings themselves, but also of the causes of the feelings and the circumstances surrounding us having these feelings. Thus, for example, we are not only unaware of many of the times that we feel fear, we are also, consequently, unaware that our fear is fear of failure, or rejection, or attack, or inadequacy, or conflict, or whatever it may be.

The whole process of avoiding bad feelings is sometimes based on the erroneous notion that we shouldn't have such feelings; that the purpose of life is to go after good feelings and to avoid bad ones. The purpose of life, I have suggested previously, is to live it, and there is only one life available for you to live; YOURS! Which means that all that is available to you, if you are to live your life, is to feel the feelings you actually have, to be in the place you are in, to do the things you are doing, and want and think whatever it is that you want and think—which includes making plans for change.

In other words, if you are actually to live your life, (rather than try to hide from it or dream aimlessly of alternatives), then you have to always be prepared to say 'yes' to whatever is in this world and in yourself. To find fulfillment, we need to give everything and anything in this world unqualified and unconditional permission to be what it already is. This really is the wisest thing that we can do, because what is *is*, regardless of whether we give it permission or not. We have to do this because it is the only starting place that is available to us. This does not mean that we become fatalists, because we also give ourselves permission to want to make all the changes in the world that we want to make, and we give ourselves permission to go off and try to make these changes. We can have the courage to try to change what we can change, but we need the grace to accept what we cannot change. Everything that *is* whatever it is at this moment cannot be changed at all; because the moment we are aware of it it has already happened. It is past and gone. All that we can influence is what *might be* in the next moment. And so every feeling that we feel now, whatever it may be, however 'bad' we think it is, needs to be unconditionally accepted. Our present feelings are part of the present moment, and nothing in the present moment, nor for that matter anything in the past, can be changed one tiny iota.

To take a simple example to illustrate what I mean; suppose I want to travel from 'A' to 'B'. At the moment I am at 'A' but I would really rather be at 'B'. In order to be able to get to 'B' I, paradoxically, have to accept that at present I am at 'A'; I have to know where I am starting from in order to be effective at getting where I want to go. Any kind of energy that is expended in wailing and gnashing against the fact of my being where I am is just a waste of energy that could be better used in getting me to where I want to be.

A full realisation of this can bring about a tremendous sense of peace beneath all the surface distraction. So much energy is wasted in trying to change what cannot be changed and fight off what already is. It is a great relief to be able to give up this foolish fight and instead focus one's energies and attention in ways that can actually produce change. A great discovery becomes possible; the realisation of the great paradox that the more one accepts what is, the more one is able to change and make changes.

Let me give some concrete examples of this in relation to the matter of having 'bad' feelings. When you repress a feeling you don't like, don't want to face, or think you 'shouldn't' have, it doesn't go away. It stays with you even though you are unaware of it, and it continues to affect what you do. For example, you might be angry or fearful in a certain situation. You avoid facing this, but the muscle tensions, stomach acid, mental preoccupations remain, and the fear or anger is quite likely to affect what you do or fail to do.

And so you haven't escaped the effects of the emotion or got rid of it; you have simply remained unaware of it. Resistance to the emotion has simply caused it to persist all the more, and nothing has been learned as a result of having the emotion.

On the other hand, suppose you managed to remain aware of the feeling of fear or anger. Suppose you accepted that you felt the emotion, didn't try to fight it, but simply became as aware of it as possible. Then you would have the chance to learn what the emotion had got to tell you about yourself, your strengths, weaknesses and the circumstances involved. You need not see the emotion as 'bad', (that would be simply to have another reaction, rejection, to the original fear and anger). Instead, you could see it simply as an opportunity to learn. You could try out different ways of behaving and become clearer about what it was that you wanted and how far you could achieve this. So, if the emotion was fear, you could test whether the fear was a useful warning, keeping you away from real danger, or an emotion that need not prevent behaviour.

If the emotion was anger you could, again, go into the source of this and find out more deeply what was happening. Thus you might observe that your anger was mainly, in your view, arising in the context of the behaviour of someone else, and that you really did want to say to this other person what you resented about them and what you wanted them to do. Or, you might discover that the anger was arising mainly after a sense of frustration about your own shortcomings, and that it looked as though you were being angry with the other person for having brought this to your attention. In other words, you were angry with the other person so as to avoid being angry with yourself.

These are just two examples of the essential principle that when we let ourselves be aware of our emotions, we can see them as opportunities to learn more about ourselves rather than seeing them as snags. We can find out what we want, what is happening to us, and what is going on all around us. As a result of this our actions can be all the more sure and informed and we can actually continue to learn instead of remaining stuck with our old prejudices.

It may seem hard to believe, but most of the pain arising from a so-called 'bad' emotion comes not from the emotion itself but rather from our futile attempts to resist it. Our 'good' times are cut short as a result of our trying to cling to them, and our 'bad' times are extended and made worse as a result of our trying to push them away. A tremendous sense of peace can come once you give up fighting whatever emotions you may have and simply let them be. It's not terrible to feel depressed, anxious, confused, heartbroken, empty, withdrawn, frightened, disappointed, despairing, insecure, at war with oneself; it's simply 'what is happening now' or the next thing to be done. Fulfillment can come from learning from the 'bad' emotions just as it comes from learning from the 'good' ones. This is not to say that we indulge ourselves in either the 'good' or 'bad' ones, but that we face up to and accept whichever ones we actually do have. At some stage we have to just accept; otherwise we feel bad about feeling bad about feeling bad about feeling bad and so on, potentially ad infinitum.

Listening

If you go out and ask friends or strangers for their advice or for their opinions, you are very likely to find that, on the whole, they are only too pleased to give them to you. Indeed, many people will be extremely keen to give you their opinions and advice long before you have ever asked for it, and will continue to give it even if you don't want it and never did want it. There is an enormous glut of advice, both good and bad.

On the other hand, try going out and asking anyone, friends or strangers, to listen to you – to listen to what you have to say about what you think, feel or want. You will find it much harder to get anyone really to use their ears instead of their mouth. Certainly there will be some who are prepared to listen, but you will find that more often than not even when people try to listen they are extremely poor listeners! There is, I repeat, a glut of advice; unfortunately there is a famine of good listening. This is a great tragedy because really good quality listening can often be far more powerful and helpful to all concerned than good advice!

We all know perfectly well what it means to listen. We pay close attention to what a person actually said, so that we are therefore more likely to hear it. We avoid getting caught up in what *we* would have said, or what we *expected* the speaker to say, or what we thought she *should* say. Good listening means that all our attention is on what the person is actually saying, rather than on our planning what *we* are going to say next, or reviewing what we did say, or in dreaming or attending to something else. That is good listening and, with our constantly buzzing minds that I have referred to earlier, we are most of us not very good at it. To listen well requires a still mind, and most of us do not manage to keep our minds still for very long.

There is really only one conclusive way of proving to yourself and to other people that you actually did hear what they said. This method is not that of simply making eye contact and prompting people at the appropriate moment. It is quite easy to *seem* to listen, when you prompt and make eye contact, without actually listening at all. The method that really works, known as 'active' or 'reflective' listening, consists in repeating back to the person, in your words at the appropriate moment and as briefly and concisely as possible, the heart of what it was that she was saying. This is easy to describe, but very difficult to do.

Most people, when they try to do this, discover that they often repeat back what *they* would have said, or what they think the person *ought* to have said, or what they thought they were *going* to say. The message, when repeated back, gets twisted, perhaps only slightly, but significantly enough for the speaker to feel frustrated; to feel that he or she wasn't really heard.

Quite commonly, the person repeating back what was said will add his own evaluations, or judgements, or interpretations of what was said, and quite fail to see that these did not come from the original speaker and should be kept quite separate from the original speaker's own words. As a result of this, many so-called conversations are extremely poor examples of effective communication. A person may speak, but all around her there are people mainly pretending to listen and putting most of their attention into working out what they are going to say next. "I might as well talk to a brick wall!" is a very common expression and with good cause. A brick wall, in some extreme cases, would not listen less effectively and at least it wouldn't interrupt. I can see a great future in machines programmed to repeat back in condensed form what a person had said! Even though we would know that there was no real human contact and no understanding involved, we would find it a relief to know that at least what we said was not completely lost. It is

probably for this reason that people can find it quite satisfying to fill in detailed questionnaires about themselves for
computers. The machine doesn't understand, but we feel
that it will not simply lose what we have said; it will make
a careful note of everything that we said.

The process of active or reflective listening can easily turn
into a mechanical and wooden, artificial affair. If you repeat
things back in a mechanical, word-for-word fashion, you can
sound more like a parrot or tape-recorder than a person.
Moreover, because you haven't replied in your own words,
you reveal that you haven't really understood and taken in
what was said, and so probably you weren't listening in the
first place. It is very difficult to be succinct and to repeat the
heart of what a person was saying without bringing in your
own evaluations and judgements of the content of what she
said. There again, if you are not as brief and concise as possible, you take up too much of the available time, and it is
wearisome to listen to you. And if you choose an inap-
propriate moment to reflect back what was said you will be
interrupting the person before she has finished a part of
what she was saying, and so disturb the flow of her thoughts
and feelings.

With the regular practice of active/reflective listening you
will discover just what a poor listener you are, but, with
practice and determination, you will improve. This depends,
of course, on your actually *wanting* to be a better listener and
wanting to listen to a given person at a particular time. You
do neither yourself nor others any useful service whatever if
you pretend to listen to them or 'go through the motions' of
listening when the truth is that you really don't want to
listen. Listening, I suggest, is extremely important, but it
doesn't follow from this that we should always be prepared
to listen to people on demand, or that we should try to listen
when we really don't want to. Active listening, when carried
out in this context, becomes an empty, foolish game.

However, the effect of a person who really *does* want to
listen and who really is a good listener is enormous, and certainly far larger than most people realise. When I find someone who really does pay attention to what I am saying;
who can hear me without making judgements; who will
accept me with warmth, support and understanding,

(regardless of whether or not he agrees with me), then I am more likely to open myself up to this person. As a result I can 'get things off my chest' and I can get much clearer about what it is that I think, feel and want, and clearer about what I am going to do next. The more I am with such a person, the more I am willing to go deeper into what my underlying feelings and wishes are. Because I am being accepted by somebody else, I am more able to accept myself and, slowly, I become more confident that I can take charge of my life. When a really good listener reflects back to me what I said, I tend to hear more clearly the heart of what I was saying, and I am more easily able to move on to what I want to say next. All this is, I think, true for everyone.

The more a person is able to listen effectively, the more likely it is that he will find other people willing to listen to him. This is by no means guaranteed, but others are much less motivated to break in on what you are saying if they know that you won't interrupt them when they are speaking, and that you will give them a chance to speak. Also, people are usually very grateful to have had someone listen to them and so are quite often keen to repay the listener by themselves paying attention to what he or she wants to say. They may, of course, be poor listeners despite their good intentions; but a good example can be, and often is, followed slowly by others.

When two people can both listen well then we really can have that rare event; close and effective communication. In such a situation, the superficial games and ploys, the emotions and swirling thoughts of the moment, can all start to be seen from a deeper perspective. When you really can listen, it is a sign that you can actually accept someone and allow her to be who she is regardless of your thoughts and feelings about her. When you listen, your own thoughts and feelings need to be kept to one side and in perspective. They are simply your thoughts and feelings, and you do not need to be wrapped up, swept away or preoccupied by them, for as soon as this happens your listening is impaired. In this atmosphere of acceptance, everyone's thoughts and feelings and wants can be seen with a sense of detachment and perspective; and people can take their own views and opinions without being swept away by them or lost in them.

The benefits of this are enormous. People no longer feel that they need to put on a show for others and can start to develop a very great sense of strength, peace and courage.

One of our very greatest needs is to be in genuine contact with other people. There seems to be a severe shortage of such genuine, effective contact, and this seems to have much to do with the fact that people frequently don't accept and support others as they are, and thus don't listen to others for more than a few seconds without becoming preoccupied with, and switching their attention to, their own thoughts and feelings.

Examples of un-awareness

Because people are frequently so sleepy, there are scores of behaviour patterns that they regularly adopt for themselves of which they are almost entirely unaware. A very large proportion of the talking psychotherapies consists in finding different ways of helping people discover for themselves what is going on in their lives; of bringing behaviour patterns that they are unconscious of into conscious awareness. It is a long process for a person to see just what feelings, motives, thoughts, wishes and behaviours he has been repressing and hiding away from himself. There seems to be no end to the number and variety of ploys that we will use to 'sweep things under the carpet' rather than face up to what we are doing and what is going on in our relationships with others. For example, a common manoeuvre is to deny one's own 'unpleasant' behaviours and then accuse and reject others for being like this. In this way we have our cake and eat it. We condemn ugly motives and actions in others while continuing to indulge them for ourselves. For instance, we will get furious about the aggression, selfishness and generally warlike attitude of others but then quite often fail to see our own warlike ways, and our own aggression and competitiveness.

Freud suggested quite a variety of 'defence mechanisms' (techniques for keeping the unconscious unconscious) that he saw people using, and others have been adding to the list ever since, while also offering alternative theories to Freud. There is considerable debate as to which are the best theories of personality and how one should go about assembling evidence to support any particular view. But regardless of how far you debate what particular methods people use to stay asleep, the fact that we do stay remarkably unaware of many things that are staring us in the face seems to me to be impossible to deny.

There is indeed at least one entire industry that positively depends on people remaining half asleep; the advertising industry. Most advertisements actually depend, for their effectiveness, on people not consciously noticing what devices are being used; because when you see through the way an advertisement has been put together, its hold on you is considerably reduced. For example, many advertisements work by constantly associating the product being sold with a situation where some basic human need is being met. Thus a house might be sold by associating it with a warm loving partner and family. A drink, or chocolate, might be sold by constantly associating them with the jet-setting 'in-crowd'. Cosmetics can be associated with confidence and success. Biscuits with the 'good old values of the past'. Soap with the 'coping mother'; and so on.

Advertisers long ago realised that people are not terribly excited about material products unless they can unconsciously imagine that, with the product, they will be one step nearer realising some basic human need, like belonging to the 'in group', being loved, being successful, being noticed, being warm and cosy, relaxing, having fun or excitement or sex, being respected, and so on. No advertiser can explicitly claim that if you buy his product you will meet such basic needs; first because this would be a lie, and you can't tell *bare-faced* lies in advertisements (you can only lie implicitly); and second because people would simply laugh at such an absurd claim and would never be fooled at all. Nonetheless, the advertisement often is successful because it relies on the T.V. audience and consumer being half asleep when she watches television or goes shopping. The viewer doesn't consciously notice that the suggestion is being made, "buy this and you will meet these human needs", and the shopper doesn't consciously reflect on many of her motives for buying the product. And so the process is completed; the shopper sees the product and without any awareness of motive reaches out for it.

Quite commonly people will say "This may be true for some people, but I have got far more sense than to think that I'll live happily ever after with these sweets or this soap or whatever". We are prepared to believe that others are gullible and unaware, but not that we ourselves can be taken in. The evidence of the success of a well put-together advertisement suggests otherwise.

Chapter Three. Awareness

Summary

We are 90% asleep?

"I don't need to look because I already know".

"I think, therefore I exist?" Use of thinking.

Thinking as a distraction from awareness of self and world.

Presence means *being present*.

Stilling the mind.

Grabbing at moments destroys them.

We think we *are* our minds.

Labels not the same as things.

Reflection and attention not contradictory; should be complementary.

Problem of polarisation; going to one or another extreme.

Obsession with the future. Time becomes more important because of mind's preparation for the future.

Purpose – to prepare for the future?

Too much rehearsal leads to non-participation.

The avoidance of feelings – "I don't know because I don't *want* to know".

Our purpose – to avoid 'bad' feelings?

Acceptance. Living *this* life – the only one available to us.

Having *these* feelings, and so on.

Listening.

Psychotherapies; explore the various ways of staying unaware.

Questions and Exercises

1. Sensory awareness: See how far you can become aware of what there is to see, hear, touch, taste and smell right now. Can you do this without having a running commentary of mental chatter? Can you hear your tone of voice when you speak?

2. Body awareness: How far can you become aware of your whole body and all of its parts? Do you feel 'connected' to your body, or do you (for example) feel cut off from it at the neck to some extent? Can you focus your awareness on to particular parts of your body? Can you, for example, be aware of the *sensations* in your left foot, or do you simply have a *visual image* of your left foot? Can you become aware of your body posture? The way you sit, stand and walk about? Can you become aware of the parts of your body that are more tense than is useful to you? Are you aware of your gestures, your facial expression? Are you aware of what you are feeling? Do you know what you want – right now? Are you aware of your 'head chatter'? The stream of thoughts? The fantasy? The planning? The reviewing? The idle drift from one thought to the next? Can you become aware of your breathing? (without changing it).

3. Can you "*be here now*"? That is, be present in the part of the world you are actually in without drifting off in your head to some other place?

4. Can you really appreciate an experience without chattering verbally or mentally about it; without labeling, or judging, or evaluating it, and without trying to grab and hold on to it?

5. Can you experience something without judging it as "bad" and without trying to push it away and avoid it?

6. Can you experience 'bad' feelings and circumstances as *gifts*? As opportunities to learn?

7. Are you a good listener? Are you going to practice the method of 'active' or 'reflective' listening?

8. Can you become aware of the basic human needs that are associated with consumer products in advertisements on television?

9. Can you become aware of the way television works upon you? Are you conscious of your motives when you switch it on?

10. Are you aware of the difference between a label and the thing being labelled? Between talk and the thing being talked about? Between direct experience and talking about an experience? Are you aware of the difference between attending to things in your head and attending to things in the world?

4. Assertiveness

Before you can even begin to try to be more assertive, there is one basic assumption that you need to make for yourself. This is the assumption that you have the right to think whatever it is you are thinking, to feel whatever it is you are feeling, and to want whatever it is you are wanting. Also, as a result, that you have the right to be the judge of all your behaviour and the right to take responsibility for the consequences. In other words, you are invited to give yourself quite unconditional permission to be who you are at this moment. Really, it is most wise to do this because all your past and present thoughts, feelings and wishes will be exactly what they are regardless of whether or not you 'permit' them to be that way!

Once you have given yourself quite unconditional permission to be whoever you are at this moment, it is suggested that you might also allow others this right; after all, they, also, will be their present selves whatever you or they might think about it.

This really is a crucial principle to understand. Assertiveness is all about wanting to see things change, but before you can be effective in making changes you have to be very clear about what *can* be changed and what *cannot* be changed. We can assert ourselves, we can be an influence, with regard to what might happen *next*. In other words, we can have some sort of influence over the *future*. What we cannot do is have any influence over, or make any difference to, the *past* or the *present*. The past has gone so how can anyone do anything about it? and the present has turned into the past as soon as we become aware of it! Either way, then, it has already happened, nothing can therefore be done about it. All we can do, having completely accepted the past and the present, is figure out what we can do next; figure out what influence we can have over the future – whether this be ten years or half a second ahead of us!

Unless you are able to accept the past and present for what it is you waste an enormous amount of energy; and the more you waste energy the less you have available effectively to assert yourself. In other words, people who are not very good at asserting themselves are constantly thinking "If only it wasn't like this ... I want it to be like that". On the other hand, the person who can assert himself effectively thinks, "It *is* like this; how can I help it to become like that?"

If you are in New York and you want to be in London it is quite useless to lie down like a two year old and chew the pavement, wailing "I don't want to be here, this is the wrong place, if only I wasn't here!" We would all see this as the beginnings of insanity. We would all realise that the wise and effective thing to do would be to recognise the present for what it is and find out where the airport was! (or whatever). The same principle applies for whatever other changes we wish to make. In order to be good at making changes you have to know what cannot be changed so that you don't waste energy trying to do the impossible. To repeat, the past cannot be changed. The present, the way everything is – *right now* – cannot be changed. All that we can do is have an influence over what happens *next*.

The person who becomes good at asserting himself, then, accepts far more than most of us are prepared to accept, He accepts the entire past and present. He accepts everything about the way he was and is. He accepts everything about the way other people were and are. He accepts everything that has happened everywhere in the world throughout all of history. He accepts everything that is happening – *right now*. When I say he 'accepts' it, I do not mean that he approves of it, or that everything turned out as he would have liked it. I mean, by acceptance, that he *recognises* that what was – *was*, and nothing can be done about it, and that what is – *is*.

Such acceptance, or recognition if you like, does not mean that we become fatalists. A fatalist is someone who considers that he can do nothing about the future, whereas the assertive person knows that he can have a considerable influence over what happens next, especially if he first of all recognises and accepts where he is starting from. I can get to London. But only if I first of all recognise and accept that I *am* in New York!

Accept what cannot be changed and then you will be able to learn how to assert yourself in relation to what can be changed. Not that assertiveness on its own is a desirable quality. If a person is assertive without also being *sensitive* to others then he tends to come over like a bull-dozer that seems unstoppable. No one is attracted to such a person.

However, I think it is true that the more assertive you are the more easy it will be for you to cope with assertiveness in others, because you will be less likely to be afraid that they will engulf you in some way. The unassertive person does not really like assertiveness in others because it reminds him that he does not really know how to deal with the demands made by others. The assertive person accepts assertiveness in others because he is confident that he can cope. With the strength and confidence that goes with assertiveness he is less likely to see other people as a threat and therefore more able to find compromises that both can accept. The unassertive person, on the other hand, tends to get very resentful when others start to assert what they want. This resentment is directed at the assertive other, but usually, when we do this, it is actually a resentment of *ourselves* for not being able to stand up for ourselves. We are resenting ourselves for not being able to cope with others as we would like. But we don't face up to this and instead project our resentment onto the person who triggered it off. Some people do this dozens of times every day.

Assertiveness, then, is closely connected (paradoxically) with acceptance and with a willingness to allow assertiveness in others. It is also quite frequently associated with *honesty*. The assertive person is more likely to be honest with himself and honest with others. Why? Because, quite simply, he accepts the way he is and he accepts the way others are, and so feels less of a need to repress any of this or lie about it. If a rose is a rose, then why bother to pretend that it is a lily? If I am in New York, then why pretend that I am in London? To pretend and repress and lie simply creates confusion for all of us. We struggle around in a fog and everyone's effectiveness is consequently reduced.

Needless to say, the quality of assertiveness that I am describing is extremely rare. I can *talk about* it much more easily than I can *do* it, (as with everything else)! And so, in order to understand the subject more clearly, let us look at what more usually goes on so that we can see the catastrophic results of it.

Dishonest, non-assertive relationships are extremely common. (In my more depressive moments I am inclined to think that they are the norm!). In such relationships people do not accept themselves in many respects and consequently tend to repress from awareness many of the things that they think, feel and want. Non-assertive people, ie. most of us, tend to have rather rigid views about how they and others should be, and whenever they find things in themselves that don't fit this blue-print they either repress these facts or else punish themselves with feelings of anxiety, incompetence or guilt. Similarly, when non-assertive people discover qualities or behaviour in others that is not the way they think it should be, they encourage the other person to be anxious, or to have feelings of inadequacy or guilt.

The assertive person will be inclined to talk in terms of "I *want* this..." or "I *feel* this..." or "I *think* that..." and the result is that we all know where we are with that person. The non-assertive person, on the other hand, will not have the courage to be straight and direct about what he wants. He will be neither honest with himself nor with others about what is happening. Instead, he invents a large collection of very detailed rules about how people should behave in the most specific of circumstances, and then he tries to get the other person to feel bad if she doesn't fit the rules. People, in other words, talk of 'should' instead of 'want' and they do this because when it is a question of 'want', as it usually is, the person has to assert this want and take responsibility. If you don't want to take responsibility and be assertively straight with someone, than what you can do is pretend that this personal wish is really a 'rule of nature', a 'moral issue', and therefore nothing to do with any wishes that you might have. To put it another way, the non-assertive person hides behind a vast edifice of pseudo-morality of his own making, in order to avoid having to assert himself and take responsibility for what he wants. And then, to add still further injury, he develops a vast repertoire of manipulative tricks that are designed to prey on the other person's latent insecurity and unease. He pretends that what he wants is a 'Rule of Nature' or 'Moral Imperative ordained by God' or whatever, and then proceeds to try to get the other person to feel fearful, foolish and generally bad for as long as she fails to fit in with this blue-print.

Such non-assertive relationships can become tortuously complicated, devious and confusing as each side tries to manipulate the other into feeling bad while all the time (of course) denying that they are doing any such thing. Endlessly, attempts are made to suggest that some moral issue is involved when, more often than not, it is simply a question of someone having a personal preference that she or he won't be honest about, assert and take responsibility for. Pseudo-moral principles are dragged in to the most absurdly detailed situations:

"You should come in to dinner for 7.00 p.m."

"You should switch the T.V. off now."

"You should go out with me this evening."

"You should fix this shirt."

"You should listen to me right now."

"You should do your homework."

...and on and on with millions of examples where 'should' does not, in all honesty, come into it, but where people have different preferences, values, goals and ideas and simply won't be honest about this.

It is a very valuable exercise indeed to become aware of the number of times a day that you and others say 'should' when it is really a question of 'I want...' or 'I think...' or 'I feel ...' Because we don't assert ourselves and take responsibility for our own preferences, we are constantly pretending that there is, as it were, some great 'Rule-Book-in-the-Sky' consisting of millions of detailed regulations that just happen to be in line with our (unstated) wishes and opinions. And we are constantly trying to get others to feel that they are 'bad people' when they don't fit in with this (non-existent) rule book.

As a result of this manipulation, virtually everyone goes around loaded up with vast accumulations of guilt, low self-esteem, uneasiness and insecurity as to whether or not they are doing things 'right'. Also, everyone has a vast repertoire of sophisticated ploys for getting others to feel equally bad about not being 'up to scratch' when they try to be themselves. It is a vicious cycle of manipulation leading to more and more manipulation. And everyone suffers in the end, even though we get the occasional, superficial, satisfaction of successfully manipulating someone.

Sometimes, I think it would be a good idea if the words 'ought' and 'should' were banned for a few score years or so. This is not because I want us all to be amoral; far from it; but because I think that practically all talk of 'should' and 'ought' these days is hopelessly tied up with ploys to get people to feel bad, insecure, foolish, self-punishing and so on. The kind of self-flagellation that goes on as a result of the appearance of ought and should is not what morality at its best is all about, and if these words are now so closely tangled up with such negative associations then we might do well to get rid of the words for a while and the negative associations that go with them.

This would not mean that we would all become amoral. A genuine understanding of morality never did, in any case, come from the stern authoritarian figure constantly handing out sets of rules and looking disapprovingly at anyone who didn't fit in. All that such a figure does (or ever did) is to promote fear and self-doubt and timid conformity and a tendency to encourage people to produce similar, unfriendly, disapproving, manipulative attitudes towards others. The genuine moral teacher, as far as I can see, rarely lectures or disapproves or talks of 'ought' and 'should' at all. Rather, she teaches by example, shows an unconditional support for the growth and well-being of others, allows people to be their different selves, is compassionate and forgiving about their failings and weaknesses without harking on about them, does not encourage people to feel bad about themselves, and doesn't pretend to have a final, rigid, set of rules that must apply to all people and for all time.

The great moral teacher does not pretend to have final answers to the mystery of being alive; does not pretend to have freed herself from her own personal foibles and foolishness; and attempts to learn and change without punishing herself in the process. I could go on and on about this, but, briefly, moral teaching seems to have far more to do with the way you experience the world and behave in it than it has to do with handing out lots of 'shoulds' and 'oughts'. It certainly does not seem to be morally desirable to disguise your own personal thoughts, feelings and preferences behind a veil of pseudo-morality, and use this to manipulate others into fitting in with your own wishes.

Abandoning the words 'should' and 'ought' would not mean that children could not learn what it was to act morally. On the contrary, they would be more likely to understand moral issues more quickly and at a deeper level. As soon as a child behaved in some way that others thought selfish and that did not seem to show regard for the thoughts and feelings of others, the adults, rather than saying "You shouldn't do this", could instead say something like "I/We don't like this. We want you to show more attention to us. We are getting angry with you. We think you're intruding into our lives too much. If you go on like this the consequences will be .... Please look at the effects of behaviour from our point of view as well as yours. We don't like being with you when you behave like this. We just don't like this behaviour."

If such messages were put over in a warm and supportive way more often than in a hostile and aggressive way, then the child would simply learn the facts of what is involved in living with others, without feeling hurt or defensive. The child would come to develop an interest and concern for others, and a sensitivity for the well-being of others as well as for himself, such that he would begin to realise that he actually wanted to find compromises that everyone concerned could accept; that he didn't want only to pay attention to his own personal wishes, since he wanted and needed to give and get support from others. Morality based on fear and manipulation is not morality at all; morality can only be based on love, toleration, acceptance, humility, sensitivity and empathy, and such morality has little need for 'shoulds' and 'oughts'.

It is easy, and traditional, to pretend that ethical matters transcend the personal thoughts and feelings and wishes of anyone; that, somehow, they lie beyond the particular judgements of anyone, and are thus beyond personal responsibility. In one sense this is true in that, when someone considers that something is a moral principle, he is suggesting that it is a useful guideline to help people live supportively with each other, and not simply a personal preference or whim. However, moral principles do not transcend individual judgements in the sense that it is always for individuals to judge whether any proposed moral principle really is worth adopting. Moses can come down from the mountainside with tablets of stone, or a priest can wave an old book in front of us. But it is for each of us to decide whether or not we feel the messages being conveyed are worthwhile and worth adopting as principles guiding human conduct. We have to trust our own judgement when people offer themselves up as prophets or teachers. As ever, the buck stops with each of us, and not with the Great Book or Great Teacher, because it is for each of us to decide whether or not we think that the book or the teacher really are great.

We can never escape this responsibility. If we say, "It must be so because others think so," or "It must be so because the book is very old", then it is *we* who are using numbers of people, or status, or age as considerations. We are responsible for this.

Authoritarian morality operates through fear and disapproval, and it manipulates people by encouraging them to feel wretched, unworthy, guilty and insecure. It rests fundamentally on the assumption that people are not to be trusted; that they are, underneath all appearances, selfish and self-seeking monsters who, if they were allowed to get what they really wanted, would create chaos and suffering. Actually, much of the suffering and chaos that exists arises precisely from the deep sense of personal unworthiness that authoritarian morality fosters and encourages. This sense of unworthiness is damaging, not only to the person who feels it, but also to everyone else that he or she knows, because it is not possible to like and accept others until one can learn to like and accept oneself.

Genuine morality, in my strongly held opinion, does not foster a sense of unworthiness; it does the opposite. It arises from hearts and minds that will love and accept all of humanity quite regardless of the circumstances and the behaviour of people. It is not based on the foolish and dangerous illusion that people are incapable of doing great evil. The genuine and great moral teacher knows that we are all capable of being very selfish and aggressive and cruel to others. But he or she also knows that we are all capable of great courage, sensitivity, selflessness and charity. The moral teacher knows that these are the qualities that ultimately provide support and benefit to whoever gives and receives them, and he or she also knows that they can best be fostered in people by unconditional love, and by example and forgiveness. When evil is committed, the moral teacher shows her rejection of the evil without rejecting the person who has committed it.

Every child who really learns about morality has the same experience. Such a fortunate child is brought up by parents who love and accept her unconditionally, who always look for the good in the child, who condemn the evil acts without condemning the child, and who encourage and give example rather than chastise and punish. The parents show their feelings and state their wishes honestly. They don't pretend to have all the answers and they do not posture in front of their children – setting themselves up as all-knowing wise people. But this doesn't mean that they aren't prepared to take a firm stand sometimes about what they want and what they feel about particular ways of behaving. Such parents take responsibility for having their own opinions, values and wishes, and do not pretend that the rules exist independently of people's judgements about rules. On the other hand, they neither pretend that, because of this, the rules are somehow unreal!

Such parents encourage the child to like and respect and accept himself with all his foibles and weaknesses, and the child realises that such acceptance does not mean that inertia, idleness and complacency about himself are being condoned. Mistakes, the child is taught, provide opportunities to learn, and what matters is how far the child resolves to learn and change. Self-torture is not recommended, being seen as ultimately useless to oneself and to everyone else.

Any person fortunate enough to have such a childhood accepts herself without ever being complacent about herself or blind to her own failings. She has learned by example from others, and she will teach others in the same way, without necessarily having to talk about it and without necessarily being any good at talking about it. And so we have a virtuous cycle. The good that has been brought out in a person, her capacity to support others, to be sensitive and accepting, tends to result in her bringing out the best in others. When positive attitudes and emotions radiate out from a person, they tend to bring out the positive attitudes and emotions in the rest of us. The opposite, sadly, is also true, and vicious cycles of dislike, insecurity and mistrust survive and prosper as much as the virtuous cycles.

The person who can love and co-operate, who can be sensitive to others and make compromises with them, is not making sacrifices. Such a person is not failing to get what he wants more often than the selfish person, because he realises that he actually wants to make compromises. He wants to co-operate with others, he wants to both give and to receive from others, and he realises that when he gives he gains as much as when he receives. The authoritarian moralist thinks that being unselfish is very difficult, because it is going against what one really wants. But the genuine moralist realises that compromise only seems difficult because of the very common delusion that we have, thinking that we are separate from and at odds with others. We commonly imagine that what we want is to get as much for ourselves as we can at the expense of others, such that any sort of compromise is really second best, to be merely tolerated when we cannot get away with what we want. The truth is that we cannot really find ourselves if we see ourselves as fortresses beleaguered by others. I will look at this in more detail in the chaper on "Personal Identity".

Types of manipulation that people commonly use.

There is a variety of ploys that people adopt in order to try to get you to feel bad and thus fit in with what they want, and it is worth looking at some of these techniques.

(i).   *"The Golden Book of All Good Reasons"*:
When we manage to say what we want, it will quite often happen that people will ask us *why* we want this. They want

to know what are our reasons, and this is hardly surprising. An assertive person will be quite happy to give reasons if it seems that the questioner is genuinely interested, and this shows concern and respect for the person asking for reasons. A non-manipulative questioner will accept your right to have the reasons you have, although he may also try to persuade you to change your mind and explain why he disagrees with you. All this is honest and straight and to be expected.

The manipulation comes when you meet a pseudo-moralist, who will try to imply, not simply that he disagrees with you, but that your reasons are not good enough when compared with the "Golden Book of All Good Reasons for Everything in the Universe". The pseudo-moralist will not simply and honestly say that he doesn't like your reasons, or considers that there is some faulty logic in your reasoning, or that he simply doesn't agree with you; rather he goes one stage further and tries to get you to believe that your reasons are not 'good enough' when compared with some objective standard or rule book. He then implies that you 'should', therefore, go along with him, and that you 'shouldn't' have the reasons you have.

The truth is that there is no objective measure of the quality of people's reasons, and also that it is impossible to go on forever giving reasons for our reasons for our reasons. The manipulator will try to get you to believe that there is a 'Golden Standard', and will encourage you to feel uneasy, foolish and guilty for not realising this and for not going along with what he wants.

Faced with such manipulation, it is useful to help the person see what game he is playing, if this is possible, and also to state quite assertively that you will only consider giving reasons for as long as there is no manipulation going on. In any case, your *ultimate* reason for wanting something is that you simply want it. We may not know why. Nobody needs to get a permit to want something, or a special certificate to show that their reasons are good enough.

(ii) *"If you want/think/feel this, I won't like you!"*

The assertive person realises the simple and fundamental truth that she cannot expect everyone (or anyone) to *like* all that she thinks, feels and wants. For as long as you are trying to get people to like all your actions and opinions you are doomed to frustration, if only because the people you know will be wanting opposite and contradictory things from you. Moreover, you will be perpetually at the mercy of others and their whims. You will never be able to stand on your own feet and think, feel and act for yourself.

A person may dislike your behaviour and opinions without being manipulative. The manipulation comes if he or she *uses* his dislike as a way of trying to get you to change your mind. In other words, if he tries to get you to feel uneasy and uncomfortable about the fact of his disliking your behaviour.

The non-manipulative person will dislike what you are doing without expecting you consequently to change your behaviour. Nor will she pretend to dislike *you* just because she dislikes what you are doing. A really manipulative ploy is to say "I won't like *you* if you do that, or think that." If this is just a bluff designed to get you to feel uncomfortable and, therefore, change, then it is a manipulation that you can ignore. You might even point out to the person what you think he is doing. If, on the other hand, it really is the case that the person really does dislike you after your behaviour, then you can be reasonably confident that he had no genuine and solid support for you in the first place. Love and concern for others, when it is of any real value, is not conditional on behaviour and opinions. If it is, then you are not being loved; rather, the love is for your opinions and behaviour.

In any event, the assertive person copes with other people without first having to be liked by them. The assertive person does not consider that she needs the approval of others before she can have her own opinions. The assertive person knows that, ultimately, she must be the judge of her own actions.

(iii) *"You have got to help me"*

It is generally agreed that a desirable quality in people is a capacity to empathise with others; to take an interest in their difficulties and be of help if you can. The pseudo-moralistic manipulative individual takes this perfectly acceptable principle and twists it into the claim that we should *always* be concerned with other people's wishes and difficulties, and *always* put others before ourselves regardless of circumstances and our own wishes. The manipulator then encourages you to feel bad if you show any signs of not wishing to fit in with what he wants, or if you don't desire to help him deal with the difficulties he faces.

For example, someone feels depressed. We might feel sympathy; we might want to help and, if we did, this would be considered to be charitable and generous. However, suppose that we didn't feel sympathetic and didn't want to help. Would that automatically mean that we were being uncharitable and ungenerous? Surely not! In any case, what seems like help is sometimes not help at all. When someone is constantly seeing herself as a victim and martyr it does not really help her play the role of rescuer or wrong-doer since this simply reinforces her in her victim/martyr role.

The greatest help we can give people is gently to encourage them in realising that ultimately they run their own lives and are responsible for their own actions. We are of best service to ourselves and others when we realise this.

Of course it is desirable to care for others and try to help them with their problems. But that does not mean that we must care for, and help, every manipulator we meet, immediately and on demand. The frequent result of such manipulation is that people end up pretending that they care about something when they think they 'ought' to care, while all the time not actually caring at all. Such pretense does neither ourselves nor anyone else any good whatsoever.

(iv). *"You may be wrong"*

A good manipulative ploy used against the unassertive person is that of trying to undermine her confidence in her own judgements and wishes, by suggesting that she may be mistaken, and that she cannot be certain that she is right. The less confident people are, the more they imagine that they must be utterly consistent, completely certain, and absolutely clear about what they want to do (or what they think) before they have the 'right' to do it, or think it. The person lacking confidence, who is consequently rather unassertive, fears making mistakes, and fears being accused of inconsistency, illogicality or ignorance. The more confident and assertive a person is, the more he realises that he is bound to make mistakes, however hard he tries to avoid them, and that the greatest mistake is to avoid ever risking mistakes. The assertive person knows that he can never know everything, that he cannot always be clear and consistent and that he is bound to change his mind sometimes. And so, whenever the manipulative person attempts to get him to feel bad by accusing him of any of this, the assertive person doesn't bother to defend himself and simply shrugs it off. He doesn't waste energy feeling bad about these inevitable human qualities.

If we try to be absolutely clear, consistent and certain before we act, then we will never act at all. The non-assertive and unconfident person imagines that others are far more organised, clear, certain and consistent than is in fact the case; and she imagines that all these impossible goals have to be achieved before she has the right to make judgements, state preferences, have thoughts and feelings, and take action in this world. The assertive person avoids getting entangled in such nonsensical attitudes.

Authoritarianism and Permissiveness
... *Adult-Child Relationships.*

The authoritarian adult tends to take the view that everything he or she thinks, feels and wants is in some objective and final sense Absolutely Right, and sanctioned by God, Morality, Justice or whatever. Consequently, he imagines, anything that the child thinks, feels and wants – that doesn't fit in with this – is Absolutely Wrong. The authoritarian will attempt to get others to feel bad (frightened, nervous, uneasy, self-punishing, stupid) whenever another dares to cross his path, and will use whatever devices he can think of to try to achieve this.

The permissive adult, on the other hand, to take one definition of this variously used word, takes the view that everything the child thinks, feels and wants is Sacred Holy Writ that must on no account, be blocked or opposed in any way, lest the delicate developing child-personality be damaged or distorted. Thus the permissive adult tends to feel guilty, and punishes herself, every time she has wishes, or whatever, that don't fit in with the child's. These are two extreme positions to take, of course, and few people are to be found absolutely at one end or the other of this continuum.

The assertive adult is not interested in either of these positions, nor either of these ways of looking at parent-child relationships. Adults and children, all are allowed to think, feel or want whatever it may be, without guilt, or fear or a sense of foolishness; and compromises are sought that everyone can accept more or less. *There is nothing neat, easy or straightforward* about the inevitable search for compromises that such an assertive attitude involves. We are constantly looking for a Book of Rules that will tell us exactly what to do in all circumstances. There is no such rule book. Ultimately we have to trust ourselves, stay alive to the circumstances of the moment, remain sensitive to ourselves and to others, and trust that we can make decisions and judgements, even though we will sometimes make mistakes.

Assertiveness and Ego

A common misunderstanding of assertiveness is thinking that it is all about winning battles with people. You get your way rather than someone else getting their way. You win, they lose. You come out as a better, sharper, stronger, more successful person than they do. You score points off them, but they leave your defences quite undamaged. None of this is assertiveness; rather, it is aggression, competitiveness and ego-obsession.

The ego-obsessed individual is most unhappy to face up to the fact that he is, like all human beings, full of contradictions, often unclear about his motives, illogical, uncertain and fallible. His polished, ideal image of himself excludes these, and other, less desirable qualities; and so he tends to feel vulnerable and becomes defensive when someone starts to home-in on these inevitable human features. In this way, the ego-obsessed individual is highly exposed to manipulative ploys. He can start to feel uneasy, stupid and guilty whenever anyone succeeds in drawing his attention to these bad characteristics, and he will waste endless hours in deviously trying to deny that he is guilty of such behaviour.

The ego-obsessed individual feels vulnerable and defensive whenever people manage to expose weaknesses, faults, or human foibles of any sort. Such an individual basically doesn't like and doesn't accept himself as he is, and he will become defensive and insecure when faults are spotlighted. He has a veneer of confidence and assertion which can easily be broken down when his human fallibility is exposed. The confidence and strength is basically an act, that is conditional on people not discovering, and him not facing, his inevitable human failings.

The genuinely assertive person manages to be assertive because she fundamentally accepts herself and likes herself as she really is, warts and all. She knows that she has all kinds of human foibles, and so when people start to talk of these she does not feel the need to defend herself, or deny the accusations, or feel insecure and exposed. As a result of this, people simply cannot manipulate her because she will not feel foolish or guilty when her faults are mentioned. The genuinely assertive person realises that real strength lies in facing up to and acknowledging our weaknesses; not in denying that we have any and repressing our fears.

The assertive person doesn't mind facing the truth about herself, because she is prepared to admit that there is some truth in what critics say about her, or 'a great deal of truth' in the criticisms, or even that they are 'entirely true' as far as she can see. She will even be prepared to seek out further criticisms from the would-be manipulator if it seems as though there is something new and useful to learn about herself. At no stage in any of this will she feel at a disadvantage, because her acceptance of herself is not dependent on maintaining fond illusions about her personality.

As a result, endless futile dog-fights of accusation, defensivenesss, counter-accusation and comprehensive dishonesty are avoided. The manipulator will lob over some devious, spiky accusation, and the assertive person will admit to anything about it that seems true, and honestly show her feelings about any of it that seems spiteful and malicious. She will show when she is hurt by remarks that are designed to hurt, and she will not deny accusations that seem to have some truth in them. Moreover, the assertive person will realise that manipulative accusations usually do have some truth in them, because people who know us also know our faults, and they assume that they can 'get us' by looking at genuine weaknesses rather than making entirely false charges!

The result of such honesty is that the manipulative individual gets no reward for being manipulative. He fails in his attempt to get another to feel bad about herself, and fails to manipulate the other person into changing her mind. When he hurts another person with malicious remarks he is forced to face up to the maliciousness, because the other person does not hide her hurt. Before long, the manipulative individual starts to wonder whether there might be some other, more honest and fulfilling, strategy available.

A virtuous cycle then becomes possible, rather than a vicious one. But this is very difficult to achieve because it is so easy, when we have been hurt by someone, to strike back at them with equally hurtful remarks, or try to get them to feel bad with manipulative remarks of our own. For example, we might even try to get a person to feel bad by saying, "How can you be so manipulative? Look at what you are saying!" etc. To do this is to be playing the same old game, and it is simply ironic that a person can use talk about honesty and assertiveness as a way of being dishonest and devious!

Attack creates defensiveness and only the exceptionally confident, assertive person can avoid such defensiveness. Counter-attack, equally, creates defensiveness and it takes considerable strength and perception to see this, and to see the futility of it.

When you want to persuade someone to change his mind, and you see the whole exercise in terms of attack, defence, winning and losing, then you will find that it is extremely unlikely that the other person will choose to change his mind. For, if you equate such a change as you winning, then he is likely to see it as a case of him losing and will thus do everything he can to avoid it. Even if you successfully 'hook' him into your way of doing things, by fostering his unease, you will only have created resentment in the long run, for all that in the short term you will have got what you want.

The truth of the matter is that none of us, strictly speaking, can change any person's mind at all. Only the person him or herself can do this. There are only two things we can do to encourage a person to change her mind. The first, most common approach, is to try to prey on a person's feelings of weakness and vulnerability, and get her to feel bad unless she changes, (ie. we are devious, dishonest and manipulative). The second, assertive, loving and lifegiving, approach is to simply and honestly state our own views and express our emotions, while all the while respecting the right of the other person to make up her mind for herself.

Paradoxically, people are far more likely to remain open to others and flexible if they are *not* being attacked, or manoevred against, or steam-rollered, When, on the other hand, winning, losing, victory and defeat are involved, then people tend to become highly armed and highly armoured. They develop all sorts of ways of hitting people, of breaking through their armour; and all sorts of ways of defending themselves, of building up a thick armour of their own, in order to avoid being hurt by others.

Weapons with greater hitting power create the need for thicker armour, or a greater ability to dodge and weave (or hide). This leads to the wish for still heavier and surer offensive capacity. We talk about the horrors of the arms race between the Super-Powers and other nations. Less attention is paid to the psychological arms race that goes on between individuals, although in fact they are quite closely linked, and one cannot be dealt with in isolation from the other. The damage done in either case is profound. At the levels of individuals, untold energy is wasted in this 'defence' activity, and untold hurt is repressed. Successful aggression creates a viciousness of spirit that damages the aggressor as much as the victim, cutting him off both from himself and the other. As in the warfare between nations, Truth is the first casualty, and the clouded awareness, fuddled perception and heat of strong emotion and righteous indignation put people increasingly out of touch with themselves and others. Consequently, they become less able to negotiate successfully for peace.

Much of the complexity of relationship between people is the needless complexity that arises from successive layers of devious manoevering, rather than the actual subtley and variety of human emotion. Dishonesty is layered upon dishonesty, and the truth can only start to appear after a slow unravelling of a tangled knot of lies.

Assertiveness and Toleration

The assertive individual manages to be assertive because she accepts herself as she is. The result of this toleration of her own weaknesses is that she tends to be more able to be compassionate and tolerant of the weakness of others, along with their hurtful remarks and stupidity. The assertive person knows that she will never fully achieve all the ideals she sets herself, which includes realising that she will never be the paragon of assertiveness being described on these pages! She will go on being hurtful and defensive at times, but she will at least try to face up to this and not be evasive when this is happening. Consequently, she will realise that others, too, will regularly fail to be honest and assertive themselves. She will try to achieve compromises that all parties can willingly accept, but she will appreciate that sometimes she will fail.

Assertiveness and Anger

The assertive person, accepting her human fallibility, knows that sometimes she will get angry and she will not try to repress this anger. However, being responsible, she will not pretend that others make her feel angry. She will know that she is responsible for her anger, and that she can, if she wishes, find other ways of responding, given sufficient courage and determination.

It is perfectly understandable that people sometimes get angry; anger, like any other emotion, just *is*; it doesn't need to be either condoned or condemned. However, when you really accept your anger, without becoming either righteously tied up with it or guilty about it, you can then start to look at it, see what it means, and consider whether it is doing you or anyone else any good. Frequently people get angry not so much with others and their behaviour, but rather with their own failure to respond to and deal with the other person as they wanted. Someone can behave in a way that I think is

positively obnoxious. I can easily pretend that I am angry
with them. But usually it is the case that I am angry with
myself, first and foremost. I am angry with myself because
I am not satisfied with the way I dealt with the person.
Perhaps I am angry with myself for feeling hurt by their
remarks. Or I am angry because I didn't manage to say
clearly and honestly what I wanted. Or I am angry because
I allowed myself to go along with their wishes as a result of
my own feelings of insecurity.

The more people can find ways of openly and honestly
expressing themselves and of accepting themselves as they
are, the less do they feel the need to get angry. If someone
is offensive with me but I successfully communicate what I
think, feel and want then there seems no need for much
anger. Anger seems futile. It makes me uncomfortable as I
'cook myself' with it; growing ulcers, breathing badly, tensing up all over. And it doesn't help me get through to the
other person, because the more angry I get the more likely
he is to become more defensive and close himself to what I
am saying. This is not to say that anger is wrong, merely that
often, (but not always), it doesn't do ourselves or others any
good. You are neither right nor wrong. But there are often
other ways of carrying on that are of more benefit both to you
and to the other person.

Nonetheless, once you are angry, the worst thing you can
do is repress it, for then it will simply persist and fester and
canker beneath the surface of awareness, perhaps for years.
Some people repress awareness of anger, sometimes for
decades. They might think that they have avoided it, but
then the old stimulus can reappear and they find that the
anger surfaces once again, quite intact, indeed larger and
more powerful than ever. The damage that anger can do in
terms of chronic tension, ulcers and jaundiced perceptions of
the world is all the greater when people repress awareness
of it. Anger when expressed can eventually be discharged.
The difficulty is to find ways of expressing anger – getting it
out of your system – without using it as a weapon to hurt or
manipulate other people. It is quite possible to show your
anger and rage at a person without trying to hurt him or
wanting him to feel bad. This is difficult to achieve, though,
because most of us are so used to being manipulative with

our emotions (or, for that matter, with anything else we can find!) When anger is honestly expressed, the other person is still liable to become defensive and anxious since we are all so used to having anger used as a weapon against us. However, the defensiveness will be less than it would be if you really were trying to attack the other person.

The most damaging results of anger occur when people become *righteous* about their anger. The pseudo-moralist takes the view that there is a Golden Standard that can certify whether or not a person should or shouldn't feel a given emotion at any particular time. According to circumstances, 'permission' can be given for a person to feel (say) angry.If permission is granted then the anger is held to be justified and 'right'. Hence, according to the pseudo-moralist, a person should continue to feel angry until the people and circumstances that caused the anger (or grief, or despair or whatever) change. When you start to become righteous about your emotions you are likely to be saddled with them for life, for it is frequently the case that neither people nor the world in general will change to suit you, however morally indignant you may feel about it.

Such righteousness can be terribly destructive. A person ends up in deciding that he would rather be right about his emotions than alive and fulfilled. And so he spends his entire life stubbornly clinging to anger, outrage, depression, hurt, hopelessness or despair, rather than honestly looking to see whether there might be other more fulfilling ways of passing time.

Once you think that you are morally right to feel the way you do, then you will imagine that, were you to change, you would have to admit to yourself that you had previously been wrong. And we all tend to hate admitting that we previously made a mistake!

The truth is that any emotion can be understandable once we manage to understand how it came about! But this doesn't mean that we feel the same way as the the person feeling the emotion or that we consider the emotion to be useful. The more able and willing we are to empathise with others, the more we are able to see and understand just how and why they have come to feel the way they do. We can start to see what the world looks like and feels like from the other person's shoes. This does not make her feelings right or wrong. With empathy we can start to understand; but the more we empathise the less we feel the need to make any judgements at all, and so the less do we see any point in talking about emotions being right or wrong. The crucial question centres on whether the emotions are fulfilling or not; whether people are managing to get through to each other, to accept each other, to become more aware of themselves, more accepting of differences, and more able to make compromises that all can accept.

The real problems arise when people use their emotions as weapons to hurt each other, or as devices to manipulate one another. I 'bash' you with my feelings, or else I hook, manoeuvre, disarm or unbalance you with them. I try any number of the thousands of possible ways to make you feel uneasy, foolish and self-punishing; in the hope that I can get you to do what I want. Then you do the same, and we together create layer upon layer of lies, pain and confusion. Assertiveness is about trying to get away from all this.

Assertiveness and Persistence

The unassertive person imagines that he needs permission to have the particular thoughts, feelings and wishes that he actually does have. This results in his tending to repress awareness of many of his wants and leads to a good deal of confusion and lack of clarity about what his thoughts and feelings actually are. As we start to accept ourselves we tend to become more clear about what our feelings are and more able to state these to others. However, it soon become obvious that it is not enough to state what you want just once. When you are faced with people who don't want to listen, who don't think that you should be as you are, and who are preoccupied with their own views, then it becomes necessary to be persistent in stating what you feel and want. It can often be necessary to state what you think and feel over and over again before a person really starts to hear what you are saying, and really sees that you mean what you say and do not intend to feel bad about it.

It is sometimes necessary to be extremely persistent in stating your wishes, for otherwise the other person will either not hear you or will not accept that you have any right to your views. It can be very satisfying to make sure that you are heard and respected, even if you do not actually succeed in getting what you want. An enormous amount of patience is needed in developing the skill and attitude of mind of assertiveness. Like any other significant skill or fundamental attitude, it takes a very long time to achieve the kind of competence being discussed here, and talking about and describing assertiveness is far easier than actually being assertive! We have to find a balance between, on the one hand, expecting miracles overnight, and on the other collapsing into despair and assuming that no change is possible. When we face large challenges we have to be both patient and persistent. We have to gear down and break the challenge into small component parts, so that we can go at it in manageable size pieces. This involves setting ourselves small goals that we can achieve from week to week. For example, knowing that we will not be assertive overnight, we might set ourselves a manageable goal by saying, "This week I will say what I want *twice* when I am talking to John", and allow ourselves to be satisfied with achieving just this; slowly building ourselves up from one week to the next.

With a major challenge, we can only cover a small amount of ground at a time, given our limited powers and experience, just as a lorry, when overcoming the obstacle of a large hill, must be geared down and travel up slowly. Otherwise it will try to rush the hill too quickly and will end up stalling and even rolling back down the hill. If anything, it is better to err on the side of caution and make a slower rate of progress than you are capable of, rather than make no progress at all. This is not to encourage people to go too far to a cautious extreme; the trouble is that quite commonly people take the view that they cannot change habits and well-established patterns of behaviour at all. We can, *if* we really want to.

Assertiveness and Honesty

Hopefully, it is clear by now that assertiveness is very closely linked with honesty, responsibility, awareness and acceptance. No one of these qualities can properly exist without the others, and each both supports and is supported by the others. On the question of honesty, though, it is worth pointing out that to be honest does not mean that you are going to be *intimate* with everyone. If I am honest and straight with you, then you can be confident that what I say to you is likely to be the truth as I see it. I will tend to avoid putting on a show with you, or playing games. This does not mean, though, that I will want to share with you my every thought and feeling. When people are intimate they tend, by definition, to share many of their deepest thoughts and feelings with each other. They understand each other very well and are very close. But it is quite possible to be honest without being intimate. People who are honest share with each other what they want to share, and keep to themselves everything else. There simply isn't time to be intimate with everyone; to know everyone very deeply; and the honest truth is that people simply do not wish to be intimate with everyone they meet. This does not stop us from being honest with each other. There is clearly a place for all levels of relationship, ranging from the most superficial to the most profound. I can be entirely honest with the bus conductor simply by asking for, and paying, the fare. If he starts to give me his life-story then I might well, in all honesty, show (preferably with some tact) that I am not particularly interested.

Genuinely intimate relationships are not possible without a substantial measure of honesty, and there is only real intimacy where there is honesty. But the reverse is not the case. You can be honest with people without being, or wanting to be, particularly intimate with them. This often seems to be confused, with people imagining that, if they are to be really honest, they must burden others with a continuous 'stream of consciousness' or running commentary on all their thoughts, feelings and wishes. Even in the most intimate relationship we could not tolerate such a boring and demanding torrent of self-revelation, and, on some occasions, it would be a destructive indulgence to reveal every one of our feelings and opinions to another. In any case, even to be close and involved with someone, as well as including intimacy, also requires that people leave each other alone and 'give each other space' sometimes.

Chapter Four. Assertiveness

Summary:

Basic requirements: acceptance of past and present; and acceptance of self and others. Assertiveness alone is not enough. Unattractive unless coupled with empathy. Associated with honesty. Non-acceptance leads to repression which results in lack of awareness. Pseudo-morality. Manipulators: attempt to get others to feel fearful, stupid and generally bad. The words 'ought' and 'should' and the way they have been polluted. Authoritarian morality. The importance of individual judgements of moral principles. Features of genuine morality. Co-operation does not require sacrifice. Types of manipulation. Authoritarianism and permissiveness. Assertiveness and ego. When genuinely assertive we need not defend ourselves. Attack creates defence. The folly of ego-battles. The psychological arms-race. Truth the first casualty in war. Aggression damages the aggressor as well as the victim. Assertiveness and toleration. Assertiveness and anger. Assertiveness and persistence. Honesty not the same as intimacy.

Questions and exercises:

1. Are you prepared to give The Past permission to be what it is, regardless of your thoughts and feelings about it? (You might as well because both Past and Present just *are* what they are, whatever you might think.)

2. Do you think that you have to have 'permission' before you can have a thought, feeling or wish?

3. Will you allow others their own thoughts, feelings and wishes? regardless of your own reactions?

4. Are you prepared to take responsibility for the consequences of being the judge of your own life?

5. Do you think that you need some kind of certificate to prove that your reasons are good enough?

6. Can you accept that people won't always like what you do and what you want?

7. Can you judge for yourself when you are going to fit in with what others want?

8. Can you stand up for yourself even though you know you may be mistaken?

9. Can you accept criticisms from others without feeling that this puts you at a disadvantage?

10. Can you show your feelings to others in an honest and straight manner, without trying to make other people feel bad?

11. Are you willing to practice being more assertive even though it will possibly take years to significantly change old habits? Can you find a balance between expecting miracles on the one hand, and giving up in despair on the other?

12. Can you look openly and honestly at your ineffective and destructive old habits without at the same time feeling the need to punish yourself?

13. Can you learn to stand up for yourself and be sensitive to your own needs while at the same time remaining aware of, and concerned about, the needs of others?

5. Worry, Guilt and Relaxation

How much time each day do you spend in worrying? Half your waking hours? Most of the day? Or just a small part of time? Many people, when they go to bed at night, are exhausted not so much because of all the work and activity they have been involved with, but because of all the worrying they have done. This kind of exhaustion has a stale, heavy feel to it and leaves a sickly taste. It is quite different from the exhaustion that arises from having been productively busy all day. That is a satisfactory feeling of fatigue that gives a sense of peace and well-being, and from which you can easily recover with sleep and rest. The tiredness that arises from worry doesn't feel at all fulfilling; you continue to feel knotted up inside, tense and frustrated with yourself; and relaxation, sleep and rest tend to seem difficult to achieve.

Worry can, and does, seriously damage your health. The more there is of it, the more each day seems to be a miserable and grey experience. Also, the more you worry about things, the more you tend to get into the habit of it. However, you are not 'made to' worry about circumstances; circumstances just *are*. Whether or not you worry about them is up to you. You do have a choice; you can get control over worry; but, as ever, it isn't easy and it takes time, determination and practice.

Useful and useless worry

People sometimes say, "If only I could just stop worrying altogether, then I could really enjoy life and get on with things effectively". To get rid of worry altogether is probably unrealistic and depending how you define worry, it can be thoroughly undesirable. Let me suggest the concept of 'Useful Worry'. Perhaps this isn't worry at all, because what I mean by it is the process of making plans for the future and learning from past experience. Useful worry is going on when you are rehearsing some future situation, making plans, getting yourself prepared, with the result that if, or when, this future moment arrives you will be able to function more effectively than you would have done if you hadn't planned. Equally useful are those times when you are looking back at something that has already happened to see where you did well or where you made mistakes, in order to learn from the past and thus function more effectively in the future.

Both rehearsal and review are obviously very valuable human attributes and distinguish us from other animals. Because of our big brains, we can bring before us in our minds bits of the world that are not actually present here and now, so that we can deal with them much more effectively when the moment of action comes. To a far greater extent than other animals we can rehearse the future and review the past and, indeed, our very idea of time arises from this ability. To try to avoid this sort of worry would indeed be irresponsible; it would be to wilfully refuse to make use of a very powerful tool that is available to us.

Useless worry, on the other hand, has the following characteristics: It does not help us function more effectively in the future, and it prevents us from functioning effectively in the present. Hence the frustration at the end of the day, when we feel that we have done a lot of worrying but have achieved very little.

The distinction between useful and useless worry seems to me to be a very important and valuable one to make. This is not to say that it is always easy to do this. Quite often you can start off worrying usefully about something and then slowly, you slip into the useless variety. The acid test question, always, is "Will this worrying help me to deal with something more effectively in the future?" If it won't then it is useless. It is serving no useful purpose whatsoever. (Which doesn't mean to say that you will find it easy to get rid of it!)

Even if the worry is useful, it may not be *useful enough* to be worth bothering with at a given time. Planning and reviewing are valuable activities up to a point. But at some stage you have to decide that the time for planning is over and the time for action has begun. If you continually try to improve your plans all the time you will never get going at all. There is no such thing as perfect preparation and people who, out of insecurity, try to achieve this end up doing nothing. As always, it is a question of finding the right balance between making plans and actually getting on with things. It is a difficult balance to find, and we each have to trust our own best judgement about it. People frequently get it wrong. The neurotic will endlessly plan and organise but never actually get started at all, preferring instead to hang around at the edge of life. On the other hand, others make a fetish of spontaneity; jumping in to all sorts of activity without trying to think anything out in advance at all. The result, often, is that their performance is a far more bungled and botched affair than it need have been, and they make far more mistakes and travel along many more blind alleyways than was necessary. The non-planner is certainly living in the present moment, but that moment is much more of a confusion and a mess than it need have been. The obsessive planner, on the other hand, is so concerned to get everything 'Right' when the Big Moment of Action comes that he ends up with hardly any contact with present-moment activity at all. He is lost in his head.

The Psychological Pay-Offs for choosing Useless Worry

It is not easy to get out of the habit of worrying uselessly, but an important step forward involves realising that there are many pay-offs to worrying. People often choose to become worriers because of the pay-offs; and so, if you are to cut down on worry, you need to find out whether, in your heart-of-hearts, you really *want* to. You need to see whether or not you are prepared to pay the price that is involved. And when you do this you might discover that you actually don't want to stop worrying at all, because in your view there are simply too many advantages in worrying.

This may seem an odd thing to say, but in fact it is not at

all uncommon for people to cling on to self-defeating behaviour, and such clinging doesn't simply apply to worry. People can be miserable, withdrawn, depressed, can feel desperately sorry for themselves, can be physically or mentally ill; and, although they might protest that they would do anything to escape from it all, it may well be that on balance they do not *want* to change at all. They are happy with their misery or whatever. It has too many advantages for them. They do not wish to let go of it.

Let's look at some of the pay-offs.

Worry as a way of avoiding Action

The great advantage of worry (and of many other self-defeating emotions) is that you don't actually have to *do* anything. If you are scared of action and participation, for whatever reason, then you can avoid getting involved by worrying instead. You can make yourself too busy with your worry to have time for anything else, and you can pretend to yourself that you are doing something because you are worrying. In fact, when you worry, whether usefully or uselessly, you are not actually *doing* anything at all. If the worrying is useful then you are *preparing* to do something, but the preparing is not the doing! No one gets any prizes for the quality of their plans; it is the actions themselves that count! But it is easy to pretend otherwise. People can think "I've done a lot with all this preparing that I have been doing", but they haven't actually done anything at all; they have merely been preparing to do something. Or they can imagine, "I've been really busy with all this worry", but they haven't been busy at all. They have avoided business and action by worrying instead.

And so a very useful question to ask yourself when you are worrying is "What am I avoiding *doing* right now? If I were to stop worrying, what would be the thing to do here and now?" You can then ask, "*Why* am I avoiding this? Am I scared of failure? Am I divided up inside myself about what I want to do?" Or perhaps, better still, just get on with the thing you know needs to be done!

With worry, then, we can avoid taking risks, we can avoid doing anything, we can avoid anything in the present that seems a threat or a difficulty. We can stay inactive while all along pretending that we are busy.

Worry to prove that you 'care'

Another great advantage of being a worrier is that you can pretend to yourself that worrying makes you a caring, sensitive person, and you can fool others into thinking this as well. This nonsense arises from a faulty logic that many people fall for: If you really don't care about very much, and you are very insensitive to what is going on around you, then you obviously won't spend very much time worrying. You won't worry, either usefully or uselessly, and some non-worriers certainly do seem to be callous, cold and indifferent to difficult circumstances and other people's troubles. However, it simply does not follow from this that if you *do* worry a lot it must prove that you do care a great deal. Caring and sensitivity are measured ultimately by people's actions; by what they do or don't do, and not by what they plan to do or get into an emotional state about. But it is easy to forget this, and so we get statements like, "I care for you a great deal; I've been worrying about where you've been and what you've been doing all the evening" as if worrying was going to help a person in some way. In any case, caring is not the same as interfering, and sometimes the most caring thing to do is to stop intruding on people's lives and let them get on with things on their own.

Worry as a way of gaining attention

Worry can be quite a successful way of having people pay attention to you, and to pity and feel sorry for you. "Poor so-and-so, she is so worried about ..." All of us like to get attention, but to do it by being objects of pity is a pathetic strategy. However, being pitied can be an easier road to travel than that of being fulfilled, and so it is quite common for people to choose this less strenuous, albeit less rewarding, option.

Worry as 'justifiable' behaviour

All the above pay-offs to worry add to the difficulties of trying to cut down on worrying. Perhaps the greatest obstacle, though, is that of foolish pride and self-righteousness. If you succeed in getting rid of a lot of worry then is it tantamount to admitting that your previous worrying was unecessary and that, essentially, you had been wasting your time. This can be a difficult fact to swallow, and some people would rather not face up to it at all. The same is true for many other forms of self-defeating behaviour. Often, people who indulge in it think that they are quite right to do so, that it is inevitable, that they are made to do so, that circumstances justify their misery, tragedy or whatever. In the event of this you need to swallow a great deal of pride and self-righteousness to admit that all along you were quite deluded; that you *had* been in control and had been actively choosing self-defeating and pointless behaviour, thoughts or emotions. Facing up to this can often seem too difficult; some people would rather be right than alive! Indeed, many therapists report that significant numbers of their patients do not wish to give up self-defeating behaviour at all. They just want to find new arguments for justifying it, and more comfortable ways of living with it. Anything; as long as they don't actually have to *give it up* as a waste of time for which they have some responsibility.

Worry and tension

When you worry about something, whether usefully or uselessly, there is bound to be a certain amount of tension involved. People complain about being too tense, and they often are. But the desirable alternative is not to be completely relaxed; for otherwise you would, for example, fall off your chair. The ideal, rather, is to tense up and use only those parts of the body that need to be tensed up and switched on for the job in hand; and give all the other parts of the body as much of a rest as possible. This takes an enormous amount of practice, and is made more difficult as a result of our bodies not having, as it were, caught up with the modern times we live in. They are still designed essentially, to cope with the stresses of a much more primitive era, and to deal with these we are saddled with a rather basic response mechanism known as the 'Fight or Flight' reaction.

The Fight or Flight reaction in humans and other animals

is well understood. When an animals meets its prey, or meets something that might attack or eat it, a period of prolonged physical exertion and mental altertness is likely to be needed if it is to get what it wants – whether this be a meal or freedom from injury. In order to cope with this exceptional physical and mental activity, the adrenal glands release the hormones adrenaline and noradrenaline which, along with other activity in the adrenal glands and autonomic nervous system, increase heart rate, divert blood from the skin and digestive organs to the muscles, and release sugar from the liver into the bloodstream. The animal becomes mentally very alert and is all keyed up for physical action, whether this be fighting the threat head-on or running away.

This is a very useful automatic response mechanism if you are a lion or a deer; but if you are a human being the response is more often a liability than an asset. This is for two reasons. First, because most of the threats or challenges that humans meet do not, these days, require exceptional physical activity; and so this automatic response alerts the body for action without any action actually occurring. The second reason concerns the creative power of our minds. Fight or flight reactions can and do occur in humans, not merely when there really is a threat or challenge present before them, but also at just the *thought* of challenges that there *might* be in the future or that there *had* been in the past! The deer can get very wound-up if there is a lion actually in front of it, but the poor human, especially if he is a useless worrier, can spend the entire day with adrenaline flowing around the system as a result of the mere thought of all the possible threats, demons and catastrophes that there might be coming next. The useless worrier is constantly thinking "What if.....?" or "If only....." and his body gets consequently charged up in the process. At worst, the person can be in an almost constant state of Fight or Flight readiness, when there is nothing actually to fight or run away from, and when little, if any, physical activity is required at all!

The results of such chronic tension are very damaging to physical and mental health. The person, mentally, can get into a state of almost constant fear and anxiety, which can remain even when the person has temporarily run out of things to worry about. The constant imaging of disasters that might be ahead, and of the mistakes that lie behind, can lead to a withdrawing of oneself into a psychological shell, as it were, and to an inability to move at all, coupled with the perception that everything outside is grey and threatening. The disturbance of activity in the digestive system can lead to ulcers, and the constant demands made on the heart can lead to heart trouble. In this context it is worth mentioning the example of the heart surgeon who found that when repairing chairs in his waiting room he needed only to have replaced the material in front of the seat, whereas chairs in other waiting rooms tended to be worn out much more evenly. The chronic worrier does indeed live on the edge of his seat!

Such chronic tension and depression seems to be extremely common, although whether it is more or less common than in previous centuries in recent history or in non-Western cultures is very difficult to determine. Certainly there seems to be a tendency in whatever period of history you come across, including our own time, to assume that 'things have never been so bad' and that 'we are at a crossroads of history' where 'things may either turn out greatly for the better, or (more likely) greatly for the worse'. Part of the reason for such thinking is, I think, due to the need to consider that we are living in a 'significant' time in order to bolster up our flagging sense of our own significance. A second reason is probably that of the depressive's need to think that things really are grey and terrible outside in order to justify him staying inactive and hidden away in a shell. Insofar as we all have a tendency to want to hide away behind armour, we are all reluctant to see the world as a potentially bright, sunny and supportive place, since we then feel rather silly just hiding away in a shell! Coupled with this common view that 'things are really grey and dreadful these days' is the common urge to believe that, once upon a time, there really was a Golden Age ... those 'Good Old Days gone by' or that, one day, we really will produce a society where we can all live happily ever after! Exaggerated fears about the present reinforce, and are reinforced by, unrealistic hopes for the future or fantasies about the past.

Techniques for dealing with useless worry

1. Just watch it in all its uselessness, and be kind to yourself about this. It takes quite a long time really to believe deep down that useless worry really is useless. A large part of us has got used to believing that all worry serves a useful purpose and is necessary or inevitable. Consequently, many months or years may be needed in just noticing how far your worrying is not actually helping anything, is stopping you from doing anything else, and is in fact being done by you rather than forced on you by others. Useless worry has to be seen as an optional extra that you choose to add to a situation.

2. 'One day at a time, one step at a time'. We can only do one thing at a time, and the only time that we can actually live is here and now. Therefore, ask yourself whether you have got the balance between planning and actually doing rather out of line. There is a tendency in our culture to rather over-do the rehearsing, and we chase ourselves around in ever tighter circles in the process. On the other hand, this has also occasionally thrown up movements which shift away, in reaction, to the other extreme where no thought of tomorrow and yesterday is allowed at all. For example, degenerate forms of the peace, flowers and love movements of the Sixties became extraordinarily anti-intellectual, and equated 'being alive' with switching off one's brain as much as possible in order to 'feel' and 'be'.

3. Remind yourself of the difference between fantasy and reality. A good deal of useless worry consists of fretting about threats and difficulties that there *might* be, but which don't actually exist here and now. Many of the demons that we worry about exist in our heads far more regularly than they exist in the world. If a lion bites you, then you are likely to feel pain. If you worry about a lion biting you then the pain is coming from you and not the lion. In other words, notice when you are making yourself ready to fight or fly from something that is not even there in front of you, and ask yourself whether it is worth real tensions about something that at the present moment is not even in existence before you.

4. (As an alternative to "3" above): Imagine the worst thing that can happen to you when you are beset by a worry, and prepare yourself for the worst. Then anything that actually does happen is likely to be an improvement on this worst expectation. You discover that you can survive even the worst, and that you can set about avoiding this and improving on your chances.

5. If you are worrying about some decision that you need to make, ask yourself whether you have all the facts you need to make a decision. It is folly to try to decide something before you have all the information you need.

6. On the other hand, it is also folly to continually avoid making a decision when you do have the information you need. The person who keeps putting off a decision ends up worrying about it for much longer than she needs to, simply because she leaves it hanging around for longer than necessary.

7. If you are a constant worrier, action can often be a good cure. If you really start to get on with doing things you simply won't have so much time available to worry.

8. On the other hand, if you find that you are constantly trying to avoid worry by obsessive activity, and you find that there is an underlying tension and anxiety in everything you do, then it may be more useful for you to stop running away from the problem, slow down and face up to whatever it is that you are worrying about. You turn round and confront it, as it were; and see if you can find out what your worrying is trying to tell you about yourself and what you want. In this context, the worrying can be seen as a gift. It is like the warning light on the dashboard of a car that is trying to tell you something. To stick a plaster over a warning light that was on would be seen as the height of folly. Similarly with worry, tension and anxiety. We need to ask "what does all this mean? what is going on here? what changes do I need to make to deal with this?"

9. It is very easy to lose all perspective when you are worrying about something. Therefore, see if you can step back from your worrying and ask yourself if you are just letting very small, trifling issues get on top of you. If you are, then you might like to decide just how much worrying time this

particular matter deserves. When this time runs out, leave the worrying at once and get on with something else.

10. It is quite pointless to worry about anything that cannot be changed. Nothing in the past or immediate present can be changed one jot. And so all worrying that begins, 'If only ....' is utterly useless worry.

It would be pleasant to be able to say that these techniques for dealing with worry are guaranteed to work; and that they will even work first time you try them and without any difficulty! Would that life were so simple. As always we need to persevere and be patient and accept that big changes are not usually made overnight. Also, it needs to be said that any given technique might be just what is needed in one situation or with one particular person, but then it might turn out that the very next day, or with a different personality, the technique does more harm than good. Thus it is that I suggest tactics that lead in opposite directions; some people need to stop wallowing around in their own misery and get on with doing something; others need to do the opposite, and stop frenetically racing around with 'useful jobs to be done' and face up to the worries that they have been avoiding. We simply have to use our own best judgement in deciding what methods to use. Our own best judgement is, indeed, fallible; but it is all that we have got.

Guilt

Worry, guilt and relaxation are all very closely linked, so that it is very difficult to consider one without looking at the others. Guilty feelings are a curse in our culture, and have been conditioned into us from such an early age that it takes a long time to get proper control over them. The trouble stems from degenerate versions of Christian moral teaching that preach that it is somehow Good to feel Bad. Such teaching encourages us to take the view that, at bottom, we are selfish, aggressive, heartless, miserable swine who would create chaos and destruction if we were given half a chance, and who should, therefore, be held on a very tight rein until we can be taught to keep ourselves in check. Children, it is assumed, are headed for disaster unless we

can implant in them an internal policeman called the conscience which will endlessly complain, bully and cajole the
person to try harder and to see himself as forever 'not up to
scratch'.

Given such teaching, it is hardly surprising that we often
have a low opinion of ourselves underneath all the posturing. We take the view that, "If people could really know me,
they would all run a mile and get away from me!" and we
assume at a very deep level that we should basically take an
apologetic view of ourselves; apologise for being here at all,
and be grateful for everything we have, given that we are so
unworthy and undeserving of anything. Such views, I
suggest, are utterly poisonous and destructive. They involve
an essentially unloving and unaccepting attitude towards
human beings, and a jaundiced propensity to focus on the
evil that people are capable of rather than a positive willingness to assume and encourage the best in people.

These negative views of humanity encourage a punishing,
judgemental view of ourselves, and they undermine people's confidence in, and love and acceptance of, themselves.
This is extremely serious, because, unless we can love and
accept ourselves as we are, we will always be at odds with
ourselves, and we will always be fearful and uneasy. The
person with true humility does not hate himself; he accepts
his weaknesses, limitations and strengths fully and unconditionally. Only by doing this can he be genuinely open to
others and realistic about what he can and cannot achieve.

The person who doesn't like himself, who constantly
punishes himself, finds it extremely difficult to show himself
to others and to face himself as he really is. Thus he is likely
to be full of evasions, avoidances and posturings. At bottom,
every ego-maniac who seems to have such a high opinion of
himself, without ever attending to his weaknesses and failings, is really without love and acceptance of himself. That
is why he is constantly trying to prove to himself and others
that he is something special, because in his heart he simply
doesn't believe it. The person with genuine humility accepts
himself as he is, and so does not need to be always trying to
prove to himself and to others that he is "O.K." The ego-
maniac, if he really did accept himself as he is, would be able
to face up to all those warts, follies, fears, and areas of

ignorance. But because he likes his *idea* of himself rather than his *actual* self he finds that he cannot face the truth.

Most of us suffer from this particular pattern of behaviour to a greater or lesser extent and, moreover, because we spend so much time moaning at ourselves, we tend to be very irritated and uncharitable when others moan at us. Such external complainings are seen as the last straw! Thus it is that we see others as tormentors when it is usually we ourselves who are most brutal to ourselves and who are our own worst enemies.

Guilt feelings, then, are too often a scourge and a curse. They have come to be equated with the 'sackcloth, ashes and hairshirt' syndrome, where we punish ourselves and see ourselves as worthless. Such behaviour is unnecessary and useless. It does neither ourselves nor others any good at all.

To make matters worse, moreover, underneath such feelings of self-torture and worthlessness, there is frequently a confusion of other feelings also present. Like resentment of the whole predicament, a feeling of sullenness, and a complex of emotions like anger, fear and despair that are repressed by the self-punishing 'guilt'. Such confusion and unawareness is extremely harmful to all concerned.

And yet it does us no good to go to the other extreme and say that we must never feel guilty. The person who doesn't love and accept himself experiences guilt as endless self-torture and it serves no useful purpose. But the person who never feels guilty at all is like a ship without a rudder; unable to keep to the course it has set itself. Guilt, in a context of love, is all about recognizing when one has done wrong and feeling consequent pangs of regret and remorse. It leads to the firmer intention to try harder to do what one considers to be right and in this way 'guilty feelings' are a valuable means by which we learn from mistakes.

As always, it is so easy to polarise in the way we think; to go to one extreme or another. Guilt without love is self-torture that serves no purpose whatever. But a complete absence of guilt, even when we had really let ourselves down, would mean that we would never learn from our mistakes and never manage to do what we thought we ought to do.

Guilt, then, is extremely valuable provided that our 'voice

of conscience' is a firm and supportive friend rather than a harsh, perfectionistic and domineering tyrant. There is a growing number of people who are heartily sick and tired of the way they have tyrannically bullied themselves for years on end. But it is sad to see some of them coming to the conclusion that therefore they will have nothing whatever to do with guilty feelings and will never feel guilty again about anything. This is to retreat to the world of the very small infant, who thinks that the world revolves around him and who knows no distinction between what he wants in this moment and what he believes to be right. The whole conception of guilt, for many people, needs to be fundamentally overhauled, but it should not be abandoned altogether.

The key that ensures that Guilt does not become corrupted and destructive is ... Love!

Guilt arises when we fail to live up to our principles or fail to achieve standards and ideas that we think we ought to have been able to achieve. When we don't do as well as we think we could, and should, have done. However, we each ultimately decide for ourselves what these standards are to be and, consequently, we are each in control of the amount of guilt we feel!

It is often difficult to assess whether we are asking too much or too little of ourselves and so, when we feel guilty, we can often wonder whether we should try harder still, or simply ask less of ourselves. Either way, it is exhilarating to realise that the guiltiness is not being thrust upon you by a demanding world, but is entirely the result of you making demands on yourself!

The same is true of many other varieties of suffering. Frequently, it is not inflicted upon us by a harsh, cruel world but, rather, it arises as a result of our desires, demands and expectations of this world. When these desires are not met, we tend to feel 'bad'. We suffer. The remedy? Well you can, of course, modify your desires and demands. If you ask for less or don't ask for anything at all, then you won't be disappointed if you don't get it!

Such a policy is taken to absurd lengths in certain decadent versions of Eastern religions, where you are encouraged to abandon all desires and expectations completely so that you can abolish suffering altogether! Such a move ignores the fact that some of our 'desires' are, more accurately, *needs*; and these, by definition, cannot be abandoned by free choice or force of will. Moreover, it is surely ridiculous to seek to avoid altogether the so-called 'negative' side of life, suffering and all, and to abandon all your desires, hopes, plans and expectations. No doubt you could reduce the pain in your life if you gave up wanting anything and wanting to change anything. But you would have also given up your personality and your humanity.

It is wise to reduce your desires when these move too far ahead of reality and what is possible. But it is escapist folly, a running away from life, involvement and commitment, to altogether abandon desire and the attempt to change ourselves and our world. It is a version of what I shall, in the next section, be calling "serenity-on-the-cheap".

Relaxation

Are you one of those people who are constantly trying to be 500 yards ahead of themselves? Are you frequently tense and jittery, rushing about like the White Rabbit in *Alice in Wonderland*? People frequently, as it were, think to themselves , "If I could just jump 500 yards ahead of myself; if I could just have an extra fifteen minutes slotted in to catch up with myself, and to get myself to where I 'should' be, then everything would be all right. I could relax then." (For a while). And so people can spend an entire day tensed up as a result of the futile attempt to catch an extra fifteen minutes. Or else people will repeatedly aim to achieve, each day, more than they know they can really achieve, and then spend the entire day punishing themselves as they slip further and further behind in the tasks they have set themselves.

What a waste of energy all this turns out to be. Why on earth don't we accept that we are precisely in the place we are in, and not half a mile or half an hour in front of ourselves? The place and time that we are in is the only place we can start to do anything, and tensing ourselves up about it is simply a waste of energy. It doesn't help us get on with whatever it is we want to do.

This kind of foolishness seems to be quite common. One

reason for this, I think, is that when people are rushing about they can reassure themselve that they must be very important and significant. "I must rush, I must get on, I must dash", people will say to each other, as if to prove that their days are full-to-the-brim with matters of great significance. We can feel somewhat uneasy if we say "Oh, no, I don't need to rush at all, there's plenty of time", because we fear that others will assume that we are being idle or that we are insignificant or that we are boasting that we can cope with less mania than others. Presumably we feel the need to prove that we are important to ourselves and others because, at bottom, we feel that we are not. A constant, frantic, dashing about can take our attention away from this feeling.

The entire English language is permeated with this mania. For example time is seen to *run* (in Spanish, I am told, it *walks*!) Time is running out, we believe; quickly, quickly, we must try to keep up with it!

Another reason why we dash about so much, and find such little peace, is that we are often in conflict with ourselves. Our minds are like a discussion group in constant uproar; with one set of voices urging us to do one thing, while others say hold back and do something else. Still further voices will say "I'm doing my best", while the oppressive voice of 'conscience' will moan and complain that you are too slow, making too many mistakes, too hesitant and so on.

The fact of such inner turmoil helps to explain a number of features of society as a whole that you might think have nothing to do with individual psychology. For example, the neurotic need to keep up with The News on T.V., radio and in the newspapers. Any journalist will tell you that for a story to become News it has to have as an ingredient either conflict, or pain, or strong emotions, or a threat to society, or scandal. In fact, it has to have as many of these as possible, with the focus set on a limited number of individuals. Journalists are quite well aware of all this but few, if any of them, pause to reflect that this indicates a serious state of mental and spiritual ill-health or dis-ease in the population as a whole. The journalist does not pause to think about this because he is too busy dashing around with the superficial dross called News, and is too busy pretending that this is all of terribly great significance.

Of course, the journalist and the reader or viewer will pretend that really the whole News-gathering madness is all about the need to be informed and to keep up with what is going on in the world. Being informed and knowing what is happening certainly are important motives, I think; but careful examination will show that the news media are very poor sources of information about anything. They may have facts, but there is little depth and understanding. Primarily, the news media exist to provide emotional excitement on the cheap, (voyeurism); a phony sense of belonging and involvement; and a source of distraction from our own inner turmoil. Information as a motive cames only after these prime considerations are satisfied, and is even displaced by the media's role as a place of ritual celebration of stereotypes and consensual values. The 'quality' press is slightly less determined by these considerations.

With the sense of depth, peace and centredness beneath the surface turmoil, that genuine relaxation can bring, the whole strange drug addiction called The News can be seen glaringly for the sorry and pathetic affair that it really is. But let's look, then, at what relaxation is and how it can be achieved.

One way of staying relaxed is to avoid getting involved in any activity whatsoever that might result in you getting tense. You can develop a thick skin, withdraw from activity, remain insensitive to the pressures and demands all around you; and the result of all this is likely to be that you will be quite calm and collected, provided also that most of your needs are being met. This is what might be called 'serenity-on-the-cheap', and I am not recommending it!

I make this point, because it ties in with the common view of relaxation that people have; namely, that it is all to do with re-charging oneself, withdrawing from the fray for a while, going un-conscious, or relatively unconscious. Certainly these are ways of relaxing, and hence it is not surprising that people tend to associate being relaxed with being asleep. For many people, the only time that they do manage to relax at all is when they are asleep.

However, relaxation can be far more than simply a recharging process, that you manage to achieve only after you have been busy. The real art of relaxation, which takes time and determination to master, involves taking a more relaxed attitude to the whole of life, so that you learn how to relax even when you are extremely busy, and not just on those few occasions when you haven't got anything else to do and so can give yourself a rest. Most of us can manage to be more or less relaxed when we are asleep, half asleep, or resting; but not so many have achieved relaxation at the same time as being wide awake, fully aware, and busy doing something.

When you are busy, a certain amount of tension, alertness and readiness is essential if you are to function effectively. The trouble, though, is that the non-relaxed person tenses muscles that do not need to be tensed; over-tenses other muscles so that they are less effective; and generally indulges in all kinds of 'busy' behaviours and mental activities that actually get in the way of the job in hand and make the person less effective. The (rare) individual who really understands relaxation does not simply avoid activity by lying and 'relaxing' all the time. She can be extremely busy, but there is a flowing, easy gracefulness about everything that she does. She neither panics, with edgy, jumpy activity; nor does she dawdle, or dither, or delay. She flows, dances, co-operates, as it were, with the activity rather than struggling, or racing, or crawling, or staggering with it. There is a tremendous economy of effort in everything she does, so that none of the tension or alertness that is involved is wasted in any way. It is all used in order to get done what is needed or wanted, and neither too much nor too little energy and attention is used.

When the person who cannot relax tries to do anything, on the other hand, whether the job to be done be large or small, he does it with an enormous waste of energy such that when the task is completed he tends to feel stale and exhausted. He has used up energy in order to complete the activity, but also he has wasted perhaps even more energy in all sorts of ways that have not helped him get the job done, and have in fact got in the way of this and actually hindered him.

Wasted mental activity can involve all kinds of fantasies of catastrophe; "What if I fail?" "What if I don't finish on time?" "What if I make a mistake?" "What if some new problem crops up?" "What if I haven't thought it all out carefully enough?" Or the wasted mental activity might involve conflict within oneself; "Do I really want to be doing this now?" "Perhaps I would be better off doing something else?" "I never really wanted to do this". A third form of wasteful mental activity can centre around regrets about the past or present situation; "It's not fair that nobody else is doing this for me"; "I wish I'd never got involved in this in the first place"; "If only I'd tried to avoid this"; "If only things hadn't turned out like this", and so on and on. All quite a waste of energy because it doesn't help get the job done or, if that is your preference, get you out of doing the job.

Wasted physical energy and activity can also be consider-able, (the mental and physical being, in any case, different aspects of the same process). A person who doesn't relax very well will tense up a variety of muscles that do not need to be tensed, and so when he acts there is a lumpy, jerky, uneven quality about what he does which hampers his effectiveness. For example, a person in a traffic jam will see the task of getting out of it as a major struggle, but in order to do this he will, if he doesn't manage to relax, indulge in all sorts of activity (physical and mental) that will not help him get out of the traffic in any way whatsoever, but which will merely serve to make him feel uncomfortable. For instance, he might grip the steering wheel very tightly, grind his teeth and keep his jaw very tense, keep revving the engine furiously even when the car isn't moving, tighten up his face into a deep frown, fail to allow himself to breathe out fully, race his heart, interfere with his digestion, tense up his shoulders, hold his legs rigidly, even tense up his stomach muscles. And none of this will help in any way whatsoever. Mental activity will include endlessly cursing that he came this way through the town, punishing himself for not antici-pating the traffic, imagining how terrible it might be if he is late, wishing that the slow-moving pedestrian would die and disappear off the face of the earth, wanting to mow down the car in front if it doesn't hurry at the next junction.

I mention traffic jams because they are an example many people are familiar with, either as motorists or passengers on a bus. But the same principles apply with every single physical and mental activity every moment of the day. It may involve something big and important, or small and trivial, but, either way, we can do it with grace, efficiency and an economy of effort, or we can struggle, strain, with a lumpy, bumpy quality and without any flow or effectiveness. We can, and do, waste vast amounts of energy in doing things that don't help complete the activity. Energy is also wasted in being at odds with ourselves, because we are still wondering whether this is really what we want or ought to be doing right now, even after we have started doing it.

In this context, it is a great breakthrough to realise that when something seems 'difficult' or 'a struggle' or 'an obstacle' it has far more to do with the *way we are dealing with the task* than with the *nature of the job itself*. Something is seen as difficult because we are not sure we want to do it, or because we are afraid of failure, or because we dislike aspects of it, and not because of anything intrinsic to the task itself. There may be something that needs to be done that is extremely complicated, time consuming, risky and repetitive. But, if we are quite certain that this is what we want to do, and we are prepared to take time, risk failure, and settle down to the repetitive aspects, then the whole task can have an effortless quality about it. We simply get on with it for as long as it takes and we don't battle with ourselves or lament how it might have been. The (very rare) person who understands relaxation to this extent, has an underlying since of peace and effortlessness underneath all the surface noise and fury. Disturbance, if it occurs, is simply accepted as that which is now involved in the activity, and so a vicious cycle of being disturbed about disturbances is avoided.

There are still further benefits to relaxation. The person who is as relaxed as possible (though not sloppy) in what she is doing, not only moves with an economy of effort, she also is much more likely to be able to see clearly what she wants to do next. She is much more able to be sensitive to what is going on within her and around her, and she is more likely to be able to listen to her own best judgements because she is not being constantly disturbed and distracted by physical tensions and skittering mental fantasies. As a result of having an underlying relaxed attitude to things, she can avoid getting caught up and carried away in moment-to-moment thoughts and feelings, and thus she is better able to make informed choices and be in control.

Relaxation techniques

It would be impossible, and pointless, to try to make a complete list of all the techniques that have been suggested to help you relax. At bottom, being relaxed involves fundamental changes in one's underlying attitudes to life which I am exploring throughout this book. However, a brief mention of techniques does seem worthwhile; as always, you have to use your own best judgement in deciding which techniques to try, and a method that might be ideal for one person at a particular place and time might be thoroughly counter-productive if tried by another person or by the same person on a different occasion. The methods can, and do, work; however no single method is guaranteed as infallible. As ever, life just isn't that simple.

1. Saying to yourself (and constantly reminding yourself): "Today I will not rush about. I will trust myself to know what is the best thing to be done, and I will do it without dithering and dawdling and without getting tense, jumpy or edgy. I will do one thing at a time, and I will not waste energy constantly wondering whether or not I should be somewhere else doing something else."

2. Imagine yourself all tensed up like a tightly-packed sack of potatoes. Then cut open the bag and let yourself flop out all over.

3. If useless tension remains and you cannot seem to be able to shift it; then just let it be, or else you will get tense about being tense (and so on).

4. The 'letting everything be' exercise. Let yourself be aware of whatever it is that you notice going on inside and outside of you. Try to avoid getting caught up with any of it. Just let it all flow by. And give everything permission to be what it is. (You might as well, because what is, *is*, whatever you may think about it).

This exercise can be done when you are not involved in any other activity, or alternatively you can do it when you are involved in some fairly humdrum or repetitive activity like washing up, walking, or simple chores of whatever sort.

5. Breathing Exercises:

a) Take a deep breath, and, as you exhale, relaaaaaaaaaa-aaaaaaaaaaaaaaaaaaaaaaaaaaaax. Repeat two or three times.

b) Push all of the air out of your stomach area and let the breathing-in take care of itself. Repeat this about half a dozen times.

c) Just be aware of how you are breathing without trying to do anything about it and without trying to breathe in any particular way. Notice how far you are not letting yourself breathe out. Notice how breathing can be allowed to take care of itself. See if you can experience not only breathing but also 'being breathed'! In one sense, breathing is something that you are doing; in another, it is something that is just happening, that is being done to you! This need not simply be a banal observation, but can have large spiritual implications, more of which later.

d) As each particular thought, emotion or tension comes along, imagine yourself, without hurry or urgency, just letting it pass away with your next breath out. As you let each breath out, let go with it your latest worry, fear or tension.

6. Create a strong fantasy of a place where you can always go, if you wish, to relax, be at peace, be calm. A place where you don't have to do anything other than just sit and stay in a state of stillness, centredness or balance within yourself. This place might be a lakeside, a beach, a temple, a warm bath; whatever fantasy works for you. (You are abusing this technique if you spend too much time at this place!)

7. See if you can get rid of, or reduce, mental chatter:

a) Imagine yourself pouring all the 'noise' out of one ear!

b) Imagine all noise and tension pouring out from your fingers and toes, with the help of a cleaning fluid. (Make this the colour, consistency and temperature that you think will work best). Imagine the level of this liquid steadily going down until all the tension is drained out.

c) Imagine yourself at a place where you can be silent. Stay there and relax and be at peace until it is time for you to move on.

d) See if you can just quietly and actively contemplate one object or sound. Choose something with shape, colours or sound that encourages a sense of peace and calm. When you find yourself distracted by passing thoughts and sensations, just calmly and gently bring back your attention to the chosen object. When you have some success with this concentration exercise you will come to realise that concentration is not the process of furrowing your brow, frowning and taking a firm grip of yourself. It is not all about holding yourself in against that part of you that doesn't want to concentrate. That is not concentration at all, but, rather, conflict within oneself and tension and wave making as a result of trying so hard to concentrate.

Concentration simply involves keeping your attention on the one thing you are attending to. If, in order to try to do this, you tense youself up and battle with yourself, then this tension and battling merely serve as yet more distraction from the object of concentration.

To be effective at concentration you have to be relaxed, gentle, alert, and forever forgiving of yourself when you find that your attention has wandered. The person who succeeds in concentrating doesn't punish himself when his attention wanders (this would merely be a further distraction) but instead gently and firmly eases his attention back to the object of concentration.

8. Make a list of particular activities that tend to help you to relax. Choose one of these and do it.

9. Ask youself: "Am I being unrealistic to expect to be able to relax very much at the moment? Do I need to pay more attention to what my thoughts and feelings are trying to tell me, and then act on this in the best way that I can?" . . . In this context it is worth mentioning the story of the woman who went to see her doctor because she was feeling so unrelaxed. The doctor asked what was happening in her life, and, when she had finished giving him a sketch of the many and various crises, demands and stresses all around her, she asked what could be done about her tension. The

doctor replied that, given all the demands being made on her, he was not at all surprised that she found relaxation difficult. He suggested that she stop being so hard on herslf, and stop expecting to remain calm and implacable when faced with such difficulties.

10. Find someone you can trust with whom you can share your thoughts, feelings and secret dreams. Someone who will appreciate and value your being open with them and who (preferably) is also willing and able to share confidences about themselves with you. "A problem shared is a problem halved" – an old and true motto. Moreover, when we manage to talk things out with others we get the chance to gain some perspective on our difficulties and avoid having them take us over.

11. If there is much tension as a result of repressing emotions, see if you can find a way of releasing these emotions. Preferably, find a way of doing this without using the emotion as a weapon with which to deliberately hurt or manipulate someone else. A balance has to be found that avoids both repression of emotions and indulgence of them. The Anglo-Saxons seem to go in for repression rather than indulgence, but neither strategy is any good. When you repress awareness of an emotion, it doesn't go away. Rather, it can poisonously fester and canker beneath the surface of awareness for years on the end until something comes along that stimulates it to the surface. You then discover that the feeling has remained, as strong and as violent as ever.

Such holding-in of emotions over a period of years results in all of us building up, over our lifetime, an enormous amount of unfinished business. This consists of all the thousands of things that we wanted to feel and say and do that we didn't. All the emotions and dreams and thoughts in past relationships and encounters that we wanted to reveal but didn't. Such covered-up emotion can lead to chronic tension, made all the more frustrating because the person is frequently not at all sure what he is tense about. Moreover, such confusion about the past often means that the person cannot see very clearly what is going on in his present relationships with people. Friends and acquaintances he knows now will say and do things that trigger-off the old and hidden emotions, and he, in turn, will set off old and previously buried emotions in other people. The result can be an utter confusion of people projecting old feelings onto new situations without realising that they are doing this. The past can start to dominate the present and to cloud everyone's awareness of what is actually happening in the present. At its worst, such unfinished business results in people trying to settle the past, settle scores with people from the past, in situations and with people who have only a very slight resemblance to those of previous encounters. For example, someone might marry a woman who reminds him of his mother in order to try to get the love that he feels he didn't get from her. Someone else might burst out in anger when his partner does something that (unconsciously) reminds him of his father; the anger for the father now being thrown at the wife. And so on with countless examples. It is extraordinary to watch the extent to which many of us behave like robots; with set patterns of feeling and behaviour coming out at the press of a button as it were.

Only by becoming aware of these old patterns and their source in our past history can we start to gain control over them. Similarly, it is useful to realise that others will have all sorts of attitudes and feelings about us and our behaviour that are really not about us at all, but are the result of the person storing up repressed feelings from past situations. Our appearance or behaviour can vaguely remind the person of these old feelings and hence trigger them off again, when really they have nothing to do with us at all. A few rounds of this mutual triggering process and, if people are not aware of what is going on, they can and do find themselves in an utterly frustrating confusion of emotion heaped upon emotion heaped upon emotion.

Chapter Five. Worry, Guilt and Relaxation

Summary:

Worry and the sense of staleness and exhaustion it produces. Useful and useless worry. Idea of 'time' arising from rehearsal and review. Useful worry not always useful enough; a balance needed between rehearsal for the future and action in the present. The pay-offs of useless worry. Worry and tension. 'Fight or Flight' reaction. Chronic anxiety states. Techniques for dealing with useless worry. Guilt; a curse in our culture. Relaxation. 'Serenity on the cheap'. Relaxation more than a re-charging process. Leads to greater sensitivity and better judgement. Techniques for achieving relaxation.

6. Self, or Personal Identity

Everyone will agree that psychology must have something to do with 'Knowing Thyself', finding yourself and coming to terms with yourself; in this chapter I want to have a look at this crucial question of personal identity. Who am I? What am I?

Quite commonly, whether they are aware of it or not, people tend to see themselves as being all the 'stuff' that they 'have'; all the things that they have accumulated over the years. "I have, therefore I exist" seems to be a common motto. What is it that we think we have? Well, obviously, I am not just talking about material things like house, car, furniture and all those status symbols; although it is likely that if you took away all of a person's material bits and pieces overnight he would probably have an identity crisis, even if you did promise to reimburse him with cash. But there are lots of other, non-material, things that we think we have, all sorts of other accumulations. For example, there are all my relationships, my achievements, the good and bad experiences that I have had, the things that regularly happen to me, my thoughts and feelings and actions, my memories. All this is, as it were, put into a great swagbag called 'myself'. The more there is of this stuff that I think I have accumulated and consumed, the more there is of 'me'. And so the aim of life becomes that of getting and consuming as many things as possible so that you become more of a person. The world seems large and you feel small, and this is a frightening experience. Therefore, it is commonly supposed, the thing to do is to get as much of it under your belt as possible and thus make it ME and MINE, (or, second best, OURS and not theirs). The more you succeed in doing this, the more proud and secure and full of yourself you will be, or so it is suggested.

If you are a powerful political dictator, this wish to accumulate and consume can involve the desire to swallow up as much territory as possible and plant your flag in as many places as possible. Even if you are just an ordinary citizen, you may well think that part of who you are is that you are British or American or whatever, and so you too will be likely to imagine that you personally will have a larger individual stature the more the country manages to colonise and extend its power. 'I have, (or we have), therefore I exist'.

Different people choose different objects to accumulate as a way of defining themselves into a more substantial existence. Some will be keen on a national political identity. Others will define themselves as being part of an organisation or group. Some will prefer to define themselves as having a substantial existence because of all their material possessions. Other people will fondly identify themselves with all their ideas or emotions, or their network of friends, or their regular routine, or their attractive body, or even just the food they eat. A few will be critical of materialistic definitions of self and will seek peak experiences or special powers or great achievements. But if they then define themselves as being that which has 'had' the special experience or great achievement, then they are as much dominated by the need to accumulate as the person who is after the Rolls Royce. Moreover, if they look down on the person who wants the Rolls Royce then they are also being just as competitive as that person. "I have a better load of stuff than you; you have only got material stuff – and so I 'win'; I am better than you!"

I say all this, not as a judgement of anybody, (in any case I am as much involved in this business of accumulation as anybody else), but simply as a description of what seem to be the facts.

Seeing ourselves as 'that which I have accumulated' is closely tied up with the competitiveness that goes on between people. We define ourselves as that which we have accumulated, and we measure this by comparing with others; and so we imagine that there will be more to us if there is more in us, both in quantity and quality, than there is in others. This leads to the deeply held wish to win in some way or another; to beat other people. And we all tend to find different ways of winning. For example, in relation to you I might feel myself to be substantial by thinking that I have more material goods than you, or that I have more power or status than you, or that I have more style than you, that I am better known than you, that I am nicer than you, or more co-operative, or more egalitarian, that I have better ideas, more intelligence, that I am more unselfish, sensitive, spiritual, giving than you. The list can be extended much more.

Some people can try to win by being more of a loser than others. They can say "I am more heartbroken, more of a failure than you. I have lived in more tragic, unjust, difficult, poverty-stricken circumstances than you". Or people can say "I have more humility than you; I am less concerned about winning than you". (And so I win!)

Many psychologists, too, tend to see Self in terms of that which has been accumulated; the defence mechanisms, the personality traits, the life history, behaviour patterns, temperament, games, the early traumas. All these start to be seen as a part of who the person 'is'.

The question that needs to be asked is, *are* we really to be defined in terms of all this assorted clutter that tends to be associated with us? Is this all that we really are? Is this who we are at all? The more that you look at this question of 'Who am I?' the deeper and stranger it gets to be.

I have material goods, (or, at least, others allow me to keep them), but that is surely not who I am, because if they were all to be taken away I would still exist. I might feel wobbly and insecure, but that would still be *me*, surely, feeling wobbly and insecure? Similarly with all the other things we think we have. All of them can be, and often are, taken away from us, or they change, or we move away. And yet surely we don't cease to exist? Everything you thought you had could be stripped away from you. You could wake up and find yourself alone as a hermit in a cave. All that you would have would be your memories, and yet surely you would still exist? Even your body can, and does, age and change, and yet still you have a sense of 'you'? "Ah well," someone might say, "all this shows that, as long as I have a few things, then I can go on existing. I can go on having my ideas, beliefs, memories, thoughts and feelings, you can't take these away, and so I continue to exist."

However, look again. Do you 'have' ideas, memories and beliefs? Just look at what happens. A thought comes and then it is gone. A memory comes and then it is gone. A stream of thoughts, memories, beliefs go by, you don't even summon them, they appear and disappear without your bidding. You don't in any useful sense have them in that you can't catch them and lock them up in a box. You can only watch them go by. Sometimes, indeed, there may be no mental imaging, remembering and thinking taking place. You are not thinking at all. You are doing or watching or listening with a clear and open mind. When your mind is blank you don't go out of existence. And even if you stop being aware of anything going on, either in your head or in the world, then you still exist. You may simply be unconscious, blank, or asleep. Many people are (more than) half asleep for much of the time and yet they still exist. Who, then, am I?

The British philosopher, David Hume, made the point over 200 years ago (and some foreigners have been making it for thousands of years) that whenever he tried to observe 'himself' he never managed to discover this mystery Self. He only ever discovered ideas and impressions of the world streaming by in a constant flow. He never saw some special object called 'himself' although he did, of course, see his body and all the other things that he considered were 'his'. Self, then, if it is an object, is not an object that can be detected whole in its entirety; you can only ever detect things that (supposedly) belong to it, or things that it has done.

In the English language, Self is not so often an object in any case. It is, rather, a 'subject', and much of English grammar works on the subject-verb-object principle. The Self (subject) *does* something (verb) *to* something (object). Does this mean that who I am is what I do? In which case I am different things at different times, according to what I am doing. 'I' then becomes like the variable 'x' in algebra, taking on different values/meanings in different contexts. Or, to put it another way, what I am doing at any given time becomes a (temporary) definition of who I am at that time. For example, "I *am* listening to the trees" states both what I am doing and who I am. At that moment all that there is of 'me' is "listening to the trees". I am lost, at that moment, in the sound of the trees. That is all that there is of me. And yet in losing myself in this way perhaps I find myself? Suppose I come to for a moment and think to myself "I lost an awareness of 'me' at that moment, I was so wrapped up in the trees". Suppose I then decide that I must keep a better grip on myself. What would this mean? That I keep saying to myself, "This is 'me' listening to the trees; I'm enjoying this; it's similar to that time last year . . ., it reminds me . . ."? But then I would no longer be listening to the trees; I would simply be talking to myself.

Do we have to keep talking to ourselves or hugging ourselves in some way in order to keep us in existence? Surely this would imply an underlying insecurity and unease in the world? The more we can trust ourselves to cope, the less do we have any need to indulge in such neurotic clinging. The minute we try to grab an experience and say "this is me and mine" we find that we have lost it and replaced it merely with ideas about 'who we are'. Or, alternatively, we replace awareness of the world and participation in it with judgements, evaluations, opinions. We chatter away in our heads about the world. On the grounds, I suppose, that 'I chatter, therefore I exist'. 'I label, judge, evaluate, therefore I exist'.

To ask the question 'Who am I?' may seem strange to some readers, in that it is not the sort of question people normally go around asking; or, if they do, they tend to keep quiet about it! In one sense it can seem like an absurd question because, in a way, we know perfectly well who we are. We are familiar enough with our behaviour, our thoughts, feelings, wishes and our history. If we know enough about these then perhaps that is all that 'knowing myself' can possibly mean? Perhaps there is no entity called 'me' other than this whole collection of behaviours, this body, these experiences etc.? And yet we are still inclined to ask, "Well who is at that has these experiences? Who is the watcher? Who is it that remembers?"

This is not an empty, sterile, philosophical question to be left to a small group of academics who are paid to play around with abstractions. The notions that we have of 'Who we are' are not simply of idle, theoretical interest; they have a decided and strong impact on what goes on in practice in our everyday lives. The person who identifies himself with being American or British will tend to want to kill foreigners if he or his self-esteem is under attack. He will identify himself with Britain or America and, therefore, the country's interests with his interests. A person who identifies himself as being a socialist or a capitalist will, likewise, feel that 'he' is under attack if these ideologies are threatened or questioned.

This matter of the way people define themselves influences countless actions and discussions on all sorts of subjects. You might imagine that, in a discussion, people are all disinterested trying to seek the truth about the subject, and that they will eagerly amend their ideas as soon as evidence is presented that throws doubt over their previous beliefs. In fact, of course, this only rarely happens. More often, we tend to think that our ideas are a part of who we are and, particularly if these are fundamental ideas, we will be as loathe to lose them as we would be reluctant to lose an arm! Whether it is an arm, an idea, or a piece of rock in the South Atlantic, it is considered to be a crucial part of 'us'.

And so it is that so much discussion becomes utterly futile and hopeless. There is little open-mindedness because each mind is clinging to a set of prejudices that it does not wish to lose. To change one's mind in such ego-centred debate is considered tantamount to admitting defeat in some way. Arguments, thus, become battles that you either win or lose rather than opportunities to share and pool information. You win an argument if you manage to thrust a part of yourself (your idea) into another person. You lose it if you find that a part of yourself (your idea) is torn away from you, and a part of somebody else (their idea) is rammed into you. This entire self-defeating process, which hinders communication and prevents learning, is based on an erroneous definition of who a person is.

Such a form of stuckness does not merely happen in relation to ideas. A person might have a regular pattern of emotional response, or regular types of behaviour, or a regular routine, and if this gets to be a part of the person's definition of who she is then she will cling on to it and be most reluctant to change any of it. This can happen even

when the behaviours and feelings are destructive and unfulfilling to the person. It is quite commonly the case that we
can become attached to a wide variety of destructive
patterns. For example, a person can, underneath all
appearances, be thinking, "I've always been a martyr figure,
or victim; I've always suffered greatly, I've always been a
loser; I've always been very tense", (...or depressed or
angry or whatever it may be). "If I were to lose any of this
I wouldn't know who I was. I *am* like this. This is who I am.
If I stop being like this then a part of me will go out of
existence!"

It can be very frightening to stop clinging to these regular
old ways. If I stop operating like a robot with the same old
habits, then I have to face the fact that those features that I
thought were 'me' are simply conditions which arise and
pass away. It is as though I am faced with a void, a vacuum.
There seems to be nothing solid to hold on to. The only
(seemingly) solid entity would appear to be that which
watches the whole flow of life as it goes past me; the ideas,
the impressions and whatever else flows past the Self, like
the stream of water in a river.

Perhaps, then, that is all that Self is; namely that which
watches all the conditions of the world arising and passing
away. And yet this Self is not an object to be observed at all;
it is the subject that is doing the observing. It is not an object
or thing; it is 'no-thing'. If this is the only solid entity that
is available it certainly doesn't seem very solid. It is not even
a thing at all; it isn't 'any-thing'; but scarcely more than the
result of our subject-object grammar. And what is this grammar? Just an idea.

However, perhaps we are just too conditioned to seek
security in things. Perhaps we have mistakenly got into the
way of thinking that only material or abstract objects, fixed
and unchanging, can provide us with safety and a refuge, so
that we mistakenly try to define Self in terms of things that
don't change. It may well be that this is a fundamental
mistake and that the whole of life consists of movement and
change, with nothing in it that is fixed and final at all.
Perhaps there is no basic and unchanging stuff in the
universe, but only events, change, process, none of which
exists in isolation from everything else.

We have tended to see objects as fixed entities, and the events and processes that surround them as ephemeral and less solid. But it is more likely that (so-called) objects are merely events-that-last-a-little-longer (than the events we are most familiar with). Moreover, it would seem that no event can be understood in isolation to all the other events, and that strictly it is not even separable from them. The separation probably exists only in our minds, which artificially have to subdivide the world in order to understand it. Even the most solid objects, like mountains, continents, planets, stars and galaxies, turn out on closer examination to be events that arise and pass away, and which in fact are simply aspects of one whole interrelated process. The universe, it would seem, is like a seamless web. To understand it fully we would need to be able to apprehend it as a single totality, which is of course, given our limited brains, quite impossible. Therefore we subdivide and consider aspects of it, one tiny bit at a time. To the extent that we forget that the separations that we make arise from our limited minds then we live in delusion. We easily start to imagine that such separations – into isolated objects and events – are basic features of the universe rather than merely devices to help us understand it.

It is interesting to consider this in relation to the English language. English is based on the distinction between nouns (things or objects) and verbs (actions or processes; 'doing' words). We can easily forget that this is merely a convention and imagine that the world really does consist of 'things' that do things (events) to each other. And we imagine that each thing is a separate entity from all the other things simply because we have separate labels. On closer examination, though, it turns out that the nouns can, if you like, all be turned into verbs. The leaf on a tree is seen to be giving out water; but the tree is also giving out leaves. It is leafing, if you like. Similarly the ground and environment around the tree is giving out the tree; it is tree-ing. The bonfire is flaming; the water is waving; the earth's surface is mountaining; the universe as a whole is John Smithing and Jean Jonesing. Every noun can have 'ing' put at the end of it so that we turn it into a verb and thus see that every apparent object is (more fundamentally) an event that arises and is created from the context of the entire universe. We live on the Earth. Or, we can say that the Sun is Earthing, and that the Earth is peopling.

This is not some pointless parlour game that can pass the time when we cannot think of anything else to do. When we really understand that the universe is one whole interrelated process we start to see that we are not separate from or at odds with the universe at all. We are part of what the universe is doing. It is not that 'I watch the universe', but rather that 'the universe is I-ing'. This is a crucial insight to achieve, indeed I think that it is *the* most important insight in the whole of life. For as long as we fail to understand it we live in world of separation, delusion and needless suffering. We imagine that we are separate from and at odds with the world and we try to accumulate as much stuff around us as possible in the futile hope that this will help us feel more secure.

What I am saying here has been said before in many different ways, more often in Eastern cultures, but now increasingly in the West. It is not, I repeat, an academic issue of no interest and importance to anyone else, but rather it crucially influences the way we experience ourselves and the way we live. Some, indeed, will say that you don't really manage to sort anything out until you have come to terms with who you are. And so I want to explore this subject of personal identity some more, despite (or because of) the fact that most of what I am saying is quite contrary to our habitual ways of experiencing and thinking about things.

The universe is 'I-ing', or, to put it another way, for as long as we seek to identify Ourselves in terms of things that are fixed and unchanging then we are doomed to frustration. The fact or possibility of change will be seen as a constant threat and so we will never feel at peace. Indeed, the more stuff we accumulate around us the greater will be our underlying insecurity because we will then have more to lose. And sooner or later we will lose it, or, rather, realise that we never had it in the first place. We can delay this awareness for a very long time; some people manage to put off facing it until they are near to death. Hence the fear of death!

When we search for solidity it is as though we were trying

to seek comfort, security and identity by hanging on to the edge of a swimming pool; only to discover that our world does not consist of a pool with solid edges, but is, in fact, only water. There are no fixed and unchanging edges to cling on to; indeed *we* are not even a fixed and unchanging entity within this flux. In other words, to take the analogy of water one stage further, not only is there no fixed and unchanging edge, but there is no fixed separate and unchanging swimmer either. We are like a wave in the water rather than a swimmer in it; and this underlies just how un-separate we are from everything else.

From this it follows that the only security that there is lies in letting go of everything and trusting yourself to move and swim with flux and change, having sufficient faith in the whole business to trust that you will not drown! This involves even letting go of any fixed and final idea of 'yourself'. This may seem like giving up the ultimate security, but if we look hard enough we can see that we cannot simply be any idea of ourselves; firstly because we are constantly changing and moving on, and secondly because, in any case, we are not just an idea. In other words, the process of burrowing deeper into the question 'Who am I?' does not provide us with a Super Answer that we can cling on to, but, rather, dashes to pieces the chances of our being able to cling on to any answer at all!

Young children seem to have a need to cling on to solid objects as a source of security; these may be blankets, dummies, favourite toys and, most important, trusted adults. Adults, too, certainly show this clinging need, and we can all recognise and understand and empathise with this feeling. However, we also in our hearts know that when someone clings on to things, or people, hoping that they will always be there and never change, they are doomed to heartbreak sooner or later. The fact of change may be delayed, but it will come eventually. For example, to take the most extreme circumstances, the person you cling to will either die in your arms or you will die in theirs. This is no trivial point. Facing up to death is ultimately inseparable from, and essential for, an understanding of the mystery of life. Perhaps the most valuable communication, contact and bonding between people is not the desperate clinging sort, but rather that which accepts and allows for the inevitability of change. It is no use saying, "I can trust and feel safe if something is fixed and unchanging", because there is nothing that is so. If we are to feel secure and to trust and let go at all, it has to be in the context of change, because that is all that is available to us. This has to be true even in our closest relationships; with, for example, spouse and with children. If someone tries to cling on to you, notice how you want to move away and how you feel suffocated! Similarly, if you try to cling on to spouse or children notice how they resent it and want to break out. Perhaps this is the very final stage of growing up; being able to cope with and deal with change. If so, the evidence would seem to be that very few of us manage to grow up fully.

'Who I am', then, seems to remain something of a movement and a mystery. You can never pin it down in any final way. Words and intellect cannot seem to wrap themselves entirely around this question. Are we just, behind all the roles, achievements and activity, an emptiness? Are we just the stage or context or space in which our life happens? Is there a firm distinction that can be made between 'me' and 'not-me'? Perhaps there isn't if I am simply a part of what the world is doing. 'I' and 'it' would then seem to be all one inseparable, interconnected process.

In the end, the process of pushing harder and harder in asking such questions shows the impossibility of there being any final answer to such questions. The process of straining away with the intellect shows the limits of intellect; which is why the greatest of the creative thinkers have always been most humble people who are acutely aware of the ultimate mystery of life. They are the ones who are most conscious that what they *don't* know is immeasurably more vast than what they *do* know, and so they are most undogmatic with their ideas. On the other hand, they are also anything but anti-intellectual, being aware of what a great gift and achievement a well-developed intellect can be.

When, on the other hand, we live in, and cling to, dogma of whatever sort we end up building an (illusory) Fortress Self, full of accumulated stuff, with lots of armour. We see ourselves as separate form and at odds with the world, and we puff ourselves up with pride whenever we imagine that we have conquered some part of it. Underneath, though, we remain doomed to feelings of insecurity and unease, with the perpetual nagging fear that all that is us and ours can so easily be taken away from us. It will pass into history. Circumstances will change. Ultimately we will die. Perhaps we can comfort ourselves with the notion that, like some Black Box flight recorder in an aeroplane, our essential soul can survive the crash of death, but this is a notion that fewer and fewer people find believable or even meaningful.

What if we can simply let go and trust the fact of change and movement? Self-definition and self-fulfillment then become matters, not of accumulating, consuming and holding on; but rather of giving out, swimming, dancing, flowing, co-operating in the movement of life. Such a self is no longer weighed down by heaps of accumulated bric-a-brac, objects, ideas, habits or whatever; instead it can move and breath and act freely and openly in the world that is all around it.

Some might say, "Well, I cannot trust and be open in that way. It involves accepting a movement and change and a not-knowing that scares me". Certainly, we can and do feel scared of change. But ultimately we have no choice. Much of our suffering, indeed, comes from trying, hopelessly, to find something fixed and final in a world of change. And the evidence seems to indicate, if we can go through the barriers of fear and insecurity, and just trust, then we find that we do survive and that we are, and always have been, supported. We would not have survived for a second without this support. People can and do swim with change. Indeed, they appear to be the ones who are the most fulfilled and at peace and joyful. Another old saying comes to mind; "When you lose yourself you find yourself." But this is not a self that can be defined.

When we can really let ourselves fully into this changing life it would seem that the barriers between self and world become in many ways more hazy. We breathe, but also we are breathed. We think, and also we are thought. We live, and also the world lives through us. We can start to *experience* our interconnectedness with everything else (and not simply theorise about it). We can start to see that, all along, the world has been supporting us being here because there is no other way that we can exist. We think thoughts, but we can also observe that thoughts just come to us quite outside our control. Indeed the matter of control itself starts to be understood more clearly. The person who sees herself as separate Fortress-Ego tends to see control as being about conquering aspects of the world. But control is not about being in conflict with the world. It is not about defying Nature, being at war with it and defeating some part of it. Control, more profoundly understood, is all about learning how to be in ever closer harmony with Nature; learning to go with it, to co-operate with it, to work with it.

When you are in control, you go with what is, you know very intimately what is, and you know what contribution you can make. Control doesn't come from defying what is, it comes from accepting what is and learning how to co-operate with it. You cannot defy Nature, if only because you are a part of Nature, a part of what is happening. Thus, for example, an aircraft taking off does not defy Nature, but co-operates with aspects of Nature in order to get into the sky. The aircraft-builder doesn't wrench the aircraft from a stubborn, opposing, resisting world. He builds it as a result of going deeply into the ways in which aspects of the world work; oil, steel, air and so on. Only by co-operation and acceptance does control become possible. The aircraft-builder has to accept quite unconditionally the ways in which oil, steel air and all the rest are; for otherwise he will never build an aeroplane that can fly.

The scientist, above all, has to learn to accept what is. He may grow very emotionally attached to a theory and be fond of its elegance and the fact that it is 'his'. But the results of an experiment might show that the theory needs scrapping or amending, and the scientist has to face such facts. He is not a conquerer, he is a co-operator. He co-operates with what is, and we would do well to do the same.

A similar pattern emerges in relation to Self-control. Fortress Ego sees self-control as the process of conquering some 'bad' part of yourself that you have been fighting against. Self-control is then all about repressing parts of the self, or living according to some blue-print where a censor or internal bully is needed constantly to check and complain and punish. The controlled self thus becomes the divided self, with one part—the good—battling against another part—the bad. But how can one part of us be ultimately in conflict with another if both parts are aspects of the same process? Rather than seeing the business of self control as one of conflict, it is more useful to see it in terms of an underlying harmony, dance or symphony. This can seem very paradoxical and yet it is true. Just as the scientist gets control over Nature by accepting and co-operating with all of it; so do we obtain self-control by accepting, co-operating and going very deeply in our understanding of all aspects of ourselves.

When we do have the courage to look inside at our own thoughts, feelings and wishes, then what we find often seems anything but peaceful and harmonious. 'Myself' can often seem like little more than a battleground upon which many warring selves or sub-personalities are locked in headlong conflict. When I look inside to try to find my Real Self I find not one personality with a single and coherent set of opinions, feelings and wishes. Instead there is a chaotic 'Parliament' of contrary and contradictory opinions, desires and feelings about any one thing. For example, someone is angry with me and shouts at me. What is my response? Quite frequently there is not just one response but a riot of different responses each following closely on the heels of the last. One part of me says, as it were, "Ouch, that hurt! ...Poor me; I don't deserve this". Another part responds, "Alex, you are so hyper-sensitive to criticism; get things in perspective". Then another, "Poor thing, she is obviously in distress". Another, "I'll get her for that!" Another, "How trivial all this is; I want to get on with something else". Another, "I am so tired and angry with hearing all these argumentative voices!" Another, "It's all her fault!' and so on. Within just a few seconds I can feel hurt, irritation with myself, moral outrage and righteousness about another, compassion for another and/or for myself, anger, maliciousness and spitefulness, despair, amusement at the whole thing, impatience with myself, confusion, giddiness, sickness, pomposity and a judgemental superiority and so on, until I get tired of the whole thing and go on to something else.

It is easy, in such circumstances, to blame and attack the

other person who precipitated this internal conflict, rather than take responsibility for the fact that it is 'me' who is in conflict. My tension, like so much tension, is generated from my contradictory responses. I can release some of my tension by attacking the other; but this is no long term solution, and it results in resentment from the other.

So how do I control myself? If I try to repress any of these moods, ideas and wishes, to thrust them out of consciousness, they have a knack of hanging around beneath the surface of awareness, and my tension and confusion remains. If I say to myself, "Only one of these moods is the 'real' me, I must crush, control and ignore the others", then I find that my internal conflict and tension increases. The other opinions, desires and moods resist more strongly the more they are attacked. They are determined to have their say; they do not wish to be crushed or ignored. 'They'? Well, actually, *me*! All these 'sub-personalities' are simply different aspects of me. The plain truth is that I, like anyone else, am not always of one mind, with one opinion, emotion or desire about an event or circumstance. I sometimes have a wide range of jostling and conflicting desires, emotions and opinions about something. And, if I am to be true to myself, open and honest with myself, I need to respect and pay attention to all this cacophony. I need to see that each particular view that I am experiencing has a contribution to make, each is a part of me that deserves respect and care, each can tell me something about myself.

Ideally, (the reality is less impressive!), I respect all my various views and emotions, but I avoid being swept along or carried away by, any of them. If I do get intoxicated with one view, then I am no longer giving myself the chance to respect and attend to the others. So each thought and response gets its share of attention, but none is allowed to dominate the others and become defined as the real me. It is as though I hold a Court of Appeal inside myself. Each plaintiff gets its chance to be heard, but none is allowed to muzzle the others. The sub-personalities may squabble and fight with each other, and this tells me a great deal about what each wishes to say and do. None of this is a hindrance to awareness and decision-making; it is part of what it means to be aware and to take *informed* decisions.

Does this mean that we have to paralyse ourselves? That we have to stay frozen with indecision and torn to pieces while we argue with ourselves? The answer is, emphatically, 'no'. When the moment comes to decide, we decide. Who is this 'we' that decides? How is the decision made if we are not at one with ourselves? ...There is a great mystery to this; but if we can trust and remain open to ourselves we find that there is a stillness at the centre of the cyclone, as it were; an unseen old wise guru that can hear all the voices and moods without identifying with any of them. This is our own best judgement. It is not infallible, but it is far more reliable than we realise and, as I have said before, it is, ultimately, all that we've got. If we trust ourselves we can pay attention to all our internal conflicts, learn from them and then act in an informed way rather than in ignorance of many of our motives and moods.

In this context it is worth quoting the therapist Fritz Perls who claimed that neurosis "...is the *premature* pacification of conflicts; it is a clinch or truce or numbness to avoid further conflict". (Perls, Hefferline and Goodman, *Gestalt Therapy*, first published in the U.S.A. in 1951, now in Pelican). This is far and away different from the usual view of sanity and neurosis. We tend to think that the well adjusted person is always single minded in thought, feeling and action. He or she forges ahead with what she wants to do and scarcely ever suffers from internal divisions. Consequently we think that this is the way that *we* 'ought' to be, and so we pretend to ourselves and others that we are far more at peace and at one with ourselves than we really are. Virtually everyone puts on this front, this pretence, that they have just one opinion, just one emotional reaction, just one desire about a particular circumstance, event or behaviour. The person who shows that she is divided is looked down upon. She, we pretend, is not coping adequately. She is not decisive enough, she must be neurotic because she is divided inside herself.

Certainly there are single minded people who always go through life with a clear picture of what they think, feel and want about everything, and without any doubts, divisions or uncertainties whatsoever. But these are not necessarily strong people. It is not strong and courageous to act when you have only got one view on what to do – the decision is easy. There are no doubts or uncertainties to make the action difficult, and so you just go ahead. Real strength consists in having the courage to act even though you still have strong fears and doubts and alternative desires. Real strength does not involve crushing or ignoring the opposition and the abstentions; but it involves action notwithstanding this, because you have decided that action is needed. If we wait until we are absolutely of one mind about the desirability of a particular action then we will frequently wait forever. And so, for example, the courageous person is one who acts even though a large part of him is saying, as it were, "don't do it, I'm scared to death, you might fail, there are other things you could be doing".

One way of being calm and at peace, then, is to be insensitive to oneself and other people. If you are a fairly callous and unaware kind of person, with limited imagination, then you may find that existence is a relatively peaceful and unruffled affair, with little of the pains of conflict, confusion and doubt. But you will have obtained your peace at the expense of aliveness/awareness. You will be indulging in a version of serenity-on-the-cheap; which can be obtained either from withdrawing from the world or by stunting one's sensibilities. You beaver away, perhaps, at some restricted and limited goal, without every pausing to reflect on what you are doing and why. You may be calm and successful in your task, but you remain shallow, undeveloped, unaware. At some stage you may wake up to your insensibility or you may spend your entire life with distraction, sedation and limited aims. Society as a whole may congratulate you on the way you have coped, managed, achieved and got on with things, and you may look down on others who feel far more plagued. But developing our full humanity does not simply mean that we give ourselves and other people a quiet life. Too often, people are relatively insensible, and worship conformity and quiet at the expense of aliveness and respect. (The best novelists and dramatists have, of course, always known about and portrayed these subtleties of personality and the reality of personal conflict).

Strength and self-control, then, are to be measured by the extent to which we respect and listen to our conflicts while still finding the courage to act when action is needed. They are not to be found in those who ignore the reality of their conflicts and who pretend that they are more at one with themselves than is in fact the case. If you ignore conflict you will either permanently kill parts of yourself that deserve to be heard, or you will find that the conflict is simply exacerbated without any kind of effective resolution. In extreme cases of psychosis, these disowned parts of yourself will eventually come screaming back at you in the form of disembodied voices, hallucinations and a severely split personality. Such experiences will terrify but, even in such cases of madness, it is well to remember that the 'insane' behaviour is in fact a desperate attempt to regain the sanity lost when a crucial part of the self was disowned, split off and repressed. Madness is, frequently, the sanest thing to be done in the circumstances! Those disowned voices will sometimes go to the most 'insane' lengths in order to be heard by us. And why? Because they (we) have got something important to say to ourselves.

There is, then, a paradox to this. The more we simply accept conflict and learn from it, the more we can find peace at the heart of it all. On the other hand, the more we resent being divided inside, and identify with various warring parts of ourselves, the more we stir up the conflict to a still greater pitch of intensity. There *is* an underlying harmony. The sage is (more often than the rest of us) at peace at the centre of his 'cyclone'. He is not, however, free of all storms – unless he has really run away from himself and the world. And so don't be taken in by the spiritual teacher who always looks entirely calm and at peace and detached from everything. He is probably playing some one-upmanship game of 'holier-than-thou'. A smug assumption of 'I am more at peace than you. (And so I win)'. The teacher to trust is one who knows suffering, doubt and conflict and who knows that these will remain and return to him time after time. Ultimately, though, he remains at peace, because this conflict is 'quite all right'. It is not an obstacle to aliveness and choice. It is the very essence of aliveness and choice and we can find peace at the heart of it, rather than in running away from it. The teacher who is worth listening to is not the one who always looks impassive; I get quite irritated with such a 'smartarse'!

The good teacher needs both to look haunted at times, while also being able to show a real smile of amusement at the whole process of internal conflict. He shows us his human foibles; and does not indulge in the folly of pretending that he has transcended all folly. Hence I like the story of the Zen teacher who said, in a tone of delight and amusement, "When I attained enlightenment I discovered that I was as miserable as ever!"

This notion of acceptance does not mean approval; rather it consists in simply and calmly being prepared to acknowledge that whatever is, is, and working from there. Paradoxically, the only way you can get to the place where you want to be is fundamentally and totally to accept/ acknowledge/notice wherever it is that you are starting from. Otherwise you don't even know where to start.

We are all very familiar with experiences of the world as a place of conflict. We are less familiar with the experience of the world and of our place in it as being all one harmony that we play our part within, and this is an important discovery for us all to make. Without it, we never know what it is really to be at peace and we never really learn what control and self control mean.

"By keeping quiet, repressing nothing, remaining attentive, and hand in hand with that accepting reality – taking things as they are, and not as I wanted them to be – by doing all this, rare knowledge came to me, and rare powers as well, such as I could never have imagined before. I always thought that when we accept things, they overpower us in one way or another. Now this is not true at all."

> Patient of Jung in *The Secret of the Golden Flower*.

Chapter Six.   Self, or Personal Identity

Summary

Self as 'that which I have accumulated'. Closely connected with competitiveness. Can we 'have' anything?
Self as subject? Or is this an accident of subject-verb-object grammar? 'I', like 'x', a variable?

Getting a grip on self? ...means talking to oneself?
'I chatter, therefore I exist'?
Futile discussion when people define themselves in terms of
'their' ideas.
People get attached to emotion, behaviours, routine – even
when these are self-defeating. They become part of *me*.
The self as watcher? Is it 'no-thing'?
Are we too conditioned to seek security in things?
Perhaps there is no basic, unchanging 'stuff'?
This is not an academic debate; definitions of self affect
experience and behaviour.
Nouns can be turned into verbs, and doing this is not just a
parlour game. Objects are really events?
Nothing finally separable from any other thing.
The universe is 'John Smithing' and 'Jean Jonesing'.
Separation arises because the mind can only apprehend the
universe one tiny bit at a time.
Letting go of any fixed and final idea of 'yourself'.
We are not an idea.
Security can only come from letting go and moving with
change.
Clinging is doomed, because change is inevitable.
Acceptance of change – the final stage of growing up?
Thus few people manage to grow up.
Soul as the black box flight recorder in the aeroplane?
Self as context; the space in which your life happens.
We *can* cope with change.
When you lose yourself you find yourself.
Arbitrary divide between 'self' and 'not-self'?
Breathing and thinking, or 'being breathed' and 'being
thought'?
Control does not mean conquering Nature.
Self-control does not mean conquering 'bad' parts of
oneself; this leads to a divided self, to bullying and
censoring.
We are part of the one process.
Acceptance does not mean approval.
Acceptance means seeing that what is, is.

Questions and exercises:

1. Become aware of your breathing without trying to change
it in any way. Are you breathing or 'being breathed'?

2. Look at your face in the mirror. Is it a fixed and unchanging object or a moving and changing event?

3. Become aware of thoughts and feelings without trying to do anything with them and without getting caught up with any of them. See if you can experience them as no more nor less 'yours' than the view outside your window, or the bus passing down the street, or the water flowing down the river.

4. Think of a seemingly fixed and unchanging object like a mountain. And then remind yourself that the geologist, with his time-scales sees the Earth as a constantly moving, heaving process with a surface as active as that of a rough sea. The mountain is an event just like a wave in the sea is an event. The 'mountain-event' lasts rather longer than the wave, and so we have more time to get attached to it.

5. Similarly, remind yourself that scientists studying stars and planets and galaxies see them as interconnected events, none of which can be fully understood in isolation from the others.

6. Become aware of some of the events that you have become attached to. Are you prepared to let go of them as they pass away? We cannot stop the tide coming up the beach, nor can we stop it going out again. Similarly with all other conditions which arise and pass away. When things (events) pass away, *let them go*. Suffering arises from the futile attempt to stop the inevitable.

7. Let go of any fixed and final idea of yourself. Just trust that, if you do this, you won't fall; you won't disappear. You don't have to stick definitions into yourself in order to continue to exist.

8. Can you see that you are not and never can be a separate island-fortress in the world? Can you experience yourself as inseparable from everything else? Spend a week in which, instead of seeing 'John Smith: His great successes and failures' (substituting your own name of course), you see instead that 'The universe is John-Smithing'. Remember, we are not *on* the Earth or *in* the Universe because that implies a separation. More exactly, we are *of* the Earth which is *of* the Universe in just the same way that a flame in the bonfire is an integral part of the bonfire. It is not *on* or *in* the fire; it is

part *of* the fire, and cannot exist or be understood in isolation from the fire.

9. Notice all the times when you have imagined that you have scored *victories* or *defeats* over circumstances. Notice that, ultimately, this is an illusion, since you are just another circumstance; an integral part of an inter-related totality. How can a flame beat or be beaten by the bonfire or by other flames? They are all one process.

10. Imagine a wave in the river worrying about beating the river or being beaten by it. Imagine a wave worrying about whether or not it is immortal or whether it is better than neighbouring waves. You are just like a wave in the river. Let go and flow like that wave. You will discover harmony and strength and a sense of connectedness with everything else. You won't win and you won't lose but you will unfold. You will no longer waste energy with fears and worries based on illusions of a separate self.

11. Just listen to the arguing and conflicting voices inside yourself and learn from all of them. See them as one great orchestra and enjoy the music.

12. Look at all the conflict and arguing that goes on between people and see that this also has underlying harmonies. It is possible to see this too as one great orchestra. You make your own music within this symphony as well as you can.

7. Love

It is with a certain amount of unease that I dare to write a chapter on Love. This word has been so variously used and (more often) misused that I sometimes think it would be a good idea if we could have a moratorium on the word for twenty years or so, such that anyone heard saying it would be asked to find some other verbal of non-verbal way of expressing him or herself. Then we might avoid the endless confusion that this particular word seems to promote. Love seems to me to be just about the most difficult phenomenon to try to describe and explain. How many of us can, in all confidence, say that we know how to communicate it or that we even understand what it is! How many can say that they are often aware of and in contact with it? Still, despite all these apologies, I am going to try to write about Love, if only because I simply cannot see how we can get very far with understanding psychology until we understand it. Some have said that love is the key to many, and perhaps all, things; that when you know what love is you know who you are and what the world is in its mystery. Certainly, to my mind, a psychology that refuses to grapple with the mystery of love just hasn't properly got started on its quest at all.

Many people will say "I love you" when in fact they mean any number of other things. "I love you" can mean, "I hope you love me", or "do you love me?", or "I hope I love you", or "I feel insecure", or "I want sex with you", or "I admire you", or "I appreciate what you just did", or "I find you physically attractive", or "I am attracted to certain aspects of your personality", or "I get many of the things I want from you", or nothing, or "I'm infatuated with you", or "I'm obsessed with you", or "I need you", or "I approve of you" and so on. I doubt that I could complete this list in one page.

Certainly it can be useful to try to see what people do mean when they use these words. Sometimes, no doubt, they do actually mean "I love you"!

But what is love? Not just the love between two people living together as sexual partners; what is love in all its various forms, in all our different relationships with all sorts of people? Perhaps it is wisest to begin by looking at some of the things it gets mistaken with that it is not. For a start, I would suggest that love is not all about having to *agree* with people. You can love someone without agreeing with their opinions and values, although, if you are to *live* with them, you have got to be able to make quite a few agreements about daily routine and underlying values simply in order to be able to co-operate effectively with chores and arrangements.

Given that love does not seem to be about having to agree with people, it follows that when you find new ways in which you disagree with someone, this does not mean that you must love them the less, or even like them less. This seems obvious enough (isn't it?) as soon as it gets stated, and yet much so-called friendship and love seems to be based on having to agree with someone. At is worst it is as though people were saying "You go along with my pretences and rationalisations and I'll go along with yours, and this will mean that we are friends". Such 'friendship' seems shallow, brittle and superficial. It is not really what friendship and love are all about.

Also, surely, it is true that love is not all about judging people, or evaluating them as more or less 'good'. If someone judges me to be good, or not so good, in various different ways, I might well feel flattered or hurt, according to whether or not the judgements are favourable. Someone might rate me very highly indeed and I might feel very pleased about it. I might well want to spend a lot of time with people who have such high opinions of me. But none of this, it seems to me, is love. Applause and praise might be very enjoyable, but ultimately with these I sense that I am being judged, graded and assessed just as much as when I am being criticised. Of course, the person who judges and grades might also love as well, but the loving is not the same as the grading.

Some people will say that love is all about giving, and this, certainly, is something that must be explored. One of the snags about this interpretation is that it can easily lead to the degenerate form of thinking that, if you really love someone and want to give to them, you must in effect be a doormat in relation to them. You must never stand up for yourself, never get involved in conflict, never try to assert yourself and never even want things for yourself. Under this guise of so-called love a tremendous amount of exploitation can, and does, go on. The person who doesn't stand up for herself loses the respect of other people, and it seems more difficult to love a person if you don't respect her. In any case, showing support, concern and empathy for others does not mean that you have to repress and ignore your own wishes and needs. People, too often, take the view that it is a question of 'either-or' here. *Either* I must only be concerned about others and completely forget about myself or I must bother only with my own needs. Frankly, it seems absurd to go to either of these extremes. In fact, you cannot be of support to yourself unless you can see that this connects up with the well-being of others, and, likewise, you cannot be of support to others unless you have a fundamental respect and regard for yourself and your needs.

So often this seems to be forgotten. The so-called selfish view is that to give anything to anyone is to lose, and that therefore getting things is much better than giving. A person who believes this sees getting as the only way of gaining, and will therefore only give anything to anyone – time, attention, assistance or whatever – if he is going to get something in return. Relationships based on this principle result in the person feeling uneasy if he is receiving more than he is giving. After all, the other person might find out, and demand that the 'deficit' be cleared. And, on the other hand, if the person thinks he is giving more than he is getting he will also feel dissatisfied because, this time, he will think that *he* is 'going short' in some way and will demand repayments.

The crucial point to realise is that to give anything what-soever *in order to* get something in return is not actually giving at all; it is *investment*. I might leave money in the bank, but I am not giving it to the bank, I am investing it there. I am giving in order to receive in return and so my giving is apparent rather than real. Similarly in any kind of emotional relationship. If you are friendly with someone, or warm and supportive, or you take an interest in them in order to get anything whatsoever out of them, then you have immediately poisoned your gift. It is no longer a gift at all; it is a phony gift. You are manipulating the person; trying to use them in some way; you are trying to make an investment out of them. And so any kind of book that encourages you to be nice, or whatever, to people *in order to do well out of them* is a poisonous book, damaging to the possibilities of us having genuine and mutually supportive relations with people.

That is why we are suspicious of friendly behaviour from people that seems phony in some way. We start to ask ourselves, "where's the catch? what does she want from me? what is she trying to get out of me?" The English particularly tend to be wary of anything that seems like dishonest friendship. The hotel receptionist who says "have a nice day", or whatever pleasantry it may be, can bring a little sunshine and light into people's lives if it sounds as though it was genuinely meant. If the person doing the job is taking an honest pleasure in being friendly and helpful to people, then we can really appreciate it. But if it is not for real; if the person is merely, robot-like, repeating a formula of words that he was trained to do at some human-relations-in-business course, or is doing it just to get our custom, then we rightly feel rather betrayed and used. And we *are* being betrayed and used, regardless of whether we realise it or not.

As soon as you take an 'investor's' approach to life you have really spoilt things both for yourself and others. Maybe in the worlds of business and commerce we don't have what it takes yet to operate any differently, (that is a vast question in itself, the question of economics and ethics). But, certainly, if we apply such an investment mentality to human relations we make it impossible for us to experience the fulfillment of giving, and also we make it impossible for us to experience the joy of receiving. We immediately think either that the gift we have received is a repayment for something we have done, or we imagine that we are consequently in debt to the giver and now owe him something. If what we received really was a gift, then we don't owe the person who gave it anything at all. And if the giver more or less openly expects something in return then he wasn't giving in the first place. The person with an investment mentality might consider all this and think "I can now see that there is a great sense of satisfaction that can come from just giving. This is very attractive to me, and so from now on I will really give to people and not expect anything in return. In this way I will be able to feel this great sense of well-being, joy and satisfaction". Immediately such a person has missed it again! If you give, and never tell anyone what you have done, and never get noticed, but inside you hang on to a quiet, smug, sense of self-satisfaction, then again, you have not really given at all. You have simply been investing in spiritual well-being.

And so it is that real giving is that in which there is no expectation of repayment. Giving, when it is for real, is done for its own sake and without any expectation of reward, recognition, or return. However, this is not to say that we don't also like to *receive* from people or that we consider that giving is *better than* receiving. The notion that to give is better than to get is connected with the puritanism often found in degenerate versions of Christian teaching. The puritan assumes that people are basically unworthy and therefore don't deserve to receive gifts which, in any case, would only corrupt them still further. All that we can do, the puritan considers, is constantly remind ourselves of our unworthiness, feel a due sense of shame and guilt, and try to earn a place in Heaven. Given our lowly state, much hard work and good behaviour will be required before we are deserving of anything whatsoever.

This, as I have explored in the section on "Guilt", is a thoroughly pernicious attitude to take towards people, however obnoxious their behaviour may appear to us. How on earth can we say that it is wrong to receive, and how, indeed, could anybody genuinely manage to give anything if no one felt able to value and honestly appreciate the gift? There are all sorts of things that we want and need from other people, and there is absolutely nothing wrong with this, and nothing wrong with trying to get some of the things we want and need. The traditional puritan, however, collapses in a heap, as it were, the minute you try to give anything to him, and foams on about how he doesn't deserve the gift, that he is unworthy, that he now owes you so much, that he can never repay you, and so on. This kind of behaviour poisons the giving; turns it stale and sour; makes it heavy and uncomfortable. The person who gives does not gain credentials or an 'I.O.U.' as a result of giving. He does not become a better person. He has simply discovered an important truth about life; which is that we need both to give and receive if we are to nurture ourselves and each other; that our own well-being is ultimately not separable from or at odds with the well-being of others.

It is important to see that we each of us richly deserve all the genuinely good things we get, quite regardless of whatever 'good' or 'bad' things we have done; simply because we are human beings. When we receive, we gain, and we need to receive things, our lives and well-being depend on it. Also, when we give we gain. But the minute we give in order to gain anything we lose all. We lose the joy of giving and all our 'gains' are poisoned. And I would stand my ground against any 'Deity' that saw things differently from this.

Many sick versions of God, based on fear and lack of love, see Him as the all-judging policeman-cum-accountant. He is constantly snooping around, grading and assessing the Great Day of Judgement. He threatens to punish us for an eternity if we are not up to scratch, without ever forgiving us; and will love us only if we fulfill a demanding string of conditions. You would never invite such a 'pain-in-the-neck' person into your house and if, indeed, it were to turn out that the Universe *is* run by such a tyrant, I hope I would have the courage to stand up to Him when the time came, and state that I had no respect whatever for His morals, and that I would suffer His bully-boy punishments as best I could.

It appals me to consider how far such morally feeble gibberish is still passed off as religious teaching today. "Do good, love one another", we are told. Why? "In order to get to Heaven. You will get the big reward. You might look small on earth, but afterwards it will be you who gets the big prizes. All debts will be repaid, all injustices straightened out. Pie-in-the-sky-when-you-die." So much of what passes for moral and religious teaching is little better than this kindergarten nonsense. The person who 'loves' and 'does Good' in order to get to Heaven is simply taking out a prudent insurance policy. He is investing in a pension in the afterlife. There is nothing particularly admirable about this. The real truth, surely is that you do good because you see that it needs to be done and you are not even particularly conscious of yourself as someone who is 'doing good'. You accept injustice if it really does seem to be the case that you can't do anything to change it; and you don't try to console yourself with the feeble pretence that injustices are always redressed. You love because love is a part of your very being. If you do these things for any other (ulterior) motive, then you have simply shown that you know nothing about goodness, giving, love or justice.

Love is not conditional on people doing the 'right' things or on them providing adequate repayments. When we are genuinely loved, we receive this love quite regardless of whatever we do or fail to do. But this is not to say that the person who loves is not also prepared to speak up strongly against things he doesn't like or approve of in others. Someone who loves us may well not love all of our behaviour, but when the love is real it is always possible to separate the behaviour from the person and to condemn the behaviour without condemning the person.

Love is not blind to the fact that people are capable of great evil, cruelty and viciousness, and the person who loves will do all he can to struggle against these evils. But he will do it without condemning the loved one; without trying to make the other feel unworthy; without trying to get the person to torture himself. Love will constantly seek out and encourage the best in people. It will not be blind to people's failings, but it will not harp on about them. It will be compassionate. It will try to mend and heal rather than blame and punish or condemn.

Thus, the loving person will have her own views, values and wishes and will not try to hide these. She will be quite prepared to state her own views, but she will seek to influence others without trying to mould them. She will ultimately respect the right of others to choose for themselves, and she will not, therefore, expect others to put on a show for her, nor will she indulge in pretence with others. This means, obviously, that there will be many occasions of conflict and confusion, both between people and within any one person.

So far, all this might be taken to imply that love is involved only in intimate relationships; that love is somehow the same thing as intimacy; with being very involved and open with a person, knowing them very deeply and having a lot of communication with them. However, I don't think that love is the same thing as intimacy at all. Different types of loving relationship obviously do depend on the degree of intimacy involved. For example, we assume that a loving relationship between two partners living together will be extremely intimate. However, this is not to say that love cannot also exist in much less intimate situations. Love is not the same thing as intimacy because there clearly can be intimacy without love. And when there is, a relationship can become a nightmare battleground of manipulation, intrigue, attack, defence, dishonesty and counter-attack. In the context of love, intimate relations can be fulfilling and supportive, but there is a place for all levels of intimacy and clearly we can't be intimate with everyone; if only because there isn't time!

The degree of intimacy, then, determines the nature of a relationship, but love or the lack of love can exist at all levels of closeness. We need different sorts of relationship, at different degrees of intimacy, with a variety of people; and we thrive most when there is love underlying all these relationships. But to say that we require love and intimacy is not to say that we need any one particular person for our survival. We do need people, but as soon as we start to imagine that we need one person in particular and that our very survival depends on him or her, then the relationship can collapse into the neurotic urge to own and cling to someone. This is a very suffocating and claustrophobic experience that is not at all like love. It easily leads on to manipulative attempts to control the other person, to keep him close, and this produces an underlying lack of trust and sense of unease. The relationship then focuses on fear, insecurity and uncertainty about the future rather than positive mutual support. Ultimately, we can give more to other people, and receive more from them, when we do not lean on them; when we do not need them for our survival.

The only exceptions to this are the loving relationships between adults and the children they are caring for. Children obviously are in a relationship of dependence with adults, although this decreases steadily as the child gets older. Unfortunately, all too often, many adults set themselves up as children in relationships, and are looking for substitute parents rather than adult partners. This is simply an example of immaturity which we need not condemn but for which we can feel compassion.

There is also the matter of mutual dependence that can be found in the 'You-and-me-against-the-world' syndrome. (This is sometimes taken, mistakenly, for love in its highest manifestation.) Two people will *evaluate* or *rate* each other very highly. They judge each other as good and they become very intimate. The trouble is that they then hang onto each other for security and try to keep out everyone else. A couple in this syndrome set themselves up, as it were, in an alliance against the rest of the world. It is as though two separate 'fortress-selves' had come together and broken down the walls between them, only to make a greater combined fortress with still larger walls that exclude everyone else from warm, trusting and supportive communication. The fireside is warm, the living room is cosy, the two people are chained closely to each other; but everything outside the front door tends to be regarded with suspicion and seen as a potential threat. Such relationships are not really based on love; they rest on mutual insecurity. It is the 'love', so to speak, that exists between NATO partners as they band together for support against the imagined Soviet 'threat'.

The 'You-and-me-against-the-world' syndrome is often closely associated with another pattern or phase; that of romantic infatuation. This can be a very pleasant experience, and who ever regrets having gone through this? But it isn't necessarily the same thing as love. The person infatuated can become obsessed with the 'loved' one and even put her on a pedestal. Nothing else matters in life; the partners, when separated, live only for the time when they can be together again. They will feel light, intoxicated, as though they were floating on clouds, in ecstacy. Nobody else and nothing else is important. This stuff of which so many films are made is surely not the same as love, although love may also be involved and may develop. Such a craze for another person, by its very nature, is most unlikely to last for very long because it is usually dependent on the novelty value of being with a new person and getting to know him for the first time. Moreover, it is often followed by the somewhat less light and joyful pattern of passionate jealousy based on insecurity, clinging and desperate need. The 'bubble' depends on there being no substantial disagreements between the two romantics, and it bursts when one or other partner starts to feel a cloying taste and a sense of claustrophobia. Sooner or later, one or other partner (and maybe both) starts to feel hemmed in with the unremitting ownership claims that each begins to make of the other.

This is the romantic conception of falling in love, but there is another, much more hard-headed, approach that also, probably, hasn't got much to do with love either. I refer to what might be called the 'market-place' approach to falling in love. In this approach everyone involved implicitly calculates their 'asset value' in the social market – worked out according to how rich, powerful, confident, physically attractive, sexy, and socially skilled they are. Having worked out their own asset value, they then look around to see who constitutes the most attractive package available to them having regard to their own buying power. A person with a very high asset value will be seen as 'beyond my reach'; while someone much lower in the pecking order will be held to be 'not good enough for me'.

After a certain amount of negotiating and exploring, deals are pulled off in which each partner is more or less happy with what he/she has managed to catch, the couple then proceeds to 'fall in love'. Occasionally people will make deals that friends and family consider to be a mistake; and thus we get remarks like: "I think she could have done much better for herself", or, "He really was very lucky to catch her; but she has always underrated herself", or, "He is obviously much too good for her". None of this, surely, has got anything to do with love.

There seems to be a tendency, which is really quite extraordinarily presumptious, to believe that each of us personally knows how to love and that the difficulty about loving centres on others. If our asset value is high we think to ourselves "I can love (of course), but who *deserves* my love?" On the other hand, if we have only a very low asset value, we think, "I can love (no problem there), but who is going to love me?" And so we imagine that the real problem centres on finding someone who will love us, either as a result of our permitting this or because they condescend to do so. More thoughtful and reflective writers and thinkers have pointed out that people have got this all wrong. The big problem is not that of getting others to love us. It is, rather, that of us managing to find love within our own hearts and pouring this out to others. And if we think that this can only be done after examination to see if the other person is deserving then we have simply shown that we do not understand what love is at all.

I describe all this, not to condemn it, but in order that we appreciate that much that passes for 'love' is not actually love at all when you stop to think about it. For a great deal of the time we manage to pretend that there is love in our actions when in fact there is not. This is hard to face and we need to be very loving of ourselves while we are in the process of confronting our un-loving ways. We also need to love others when we discover the depths of their lack of love. This is pure paradox, but it is, I think, the truth. When love is described in the fairy tales, it is the love between the fairy prince and princess; both beautiful, lovely, unblemished and loving people. In fact the world is populated by 'frogs' as it were, and we had better give up hoping that, when we kiss, either we or anyone else will turn into royalty!

These fairy tale myths of frogs and princes, beauties and beasts, contain a powerful message. The ugly frog is also, underneath, a handsome prince. Not just physically handsome, but beautiful as a person. On the other hand, the attractive prince and princess also turn out to be childish, petulant, shallow and immature. They are 'frog-like' in personality if not in appearance. Within all of us, in other words, there is that which we can find beautiful and that which we will see to be ugly, cruel, vicious and all the rest. Love is not blind to the ugliness and the trail of devastation that we each leave behind us; but real love does not wait for someone to come along who 'deserves' to be loved. If you kiss an (inevitably) frog-like person because you hope to discover that he is in fact a prince you have missed the whole point of love and the whole point of this particular fairy tale. People blossom when they are embraced by others in their totality. The frog turned into the prince when the girl had accepted that he was also a frog but kissed him anyway. The beast turned into the handsome man or, rather, showed the 'handsome' side of his personality, when the woman loved him as he was – 'warts and all'.

The story of Christ's love of Man also, surely, can be used to illustrate the same principle. The degenerate version is that God will love us provided that we get rid of our ugly ways; in other words, He will love us only if we 'deserve' it, and, if we don't, we face eternal damnation. A more enlightened interpretation of this story (whether or not you think the story is true is irrelevant) states that Christ's love for us is quite unconditional on the number of blemishes in our personality. He loves us as we are right now, which is not to say that he condones our vicious ways. (More of this later).

In everyday life, of course, (so-called) love and friendship is frequently based on assessments of whether or not people are deserving. This kind of thinking occurs not just between potential couples but also in relation to cliques of all sorts and among all age groups. "I will be friends with you," people think, "because you deserve to be my friend." Or, "We will let you join our group and be friends with us because you have the right 'credentials' for entry into our group". Thus it is that we have the high status 'In-groups' that have high asset ratings; the members are powerful, or rich, or socially skilled, or physically attractive or whatever. And, inevitably, we also have the 'out-groups' of people who hang together if only because, at worst, nobody else wants to be with them.

It is probably inevitable that people will prefer to be with others who have qualities that attract them and who agree with them about many things. No doubt we will all continue to team up with others according to judgements about asset values; as a result of agreements, assessments, alliances and all the rest. But let us not confuse any of this with love.

What, then, *is* love? We still haven't managed to pin it down. I have said just a little about what it is and quite a lot about what it is not. The truth is, I think, that love is not actually any particular emotion or thought or action at all. If I say "I love you" it does not mean that I am necessarily doing or thinking or feeling anything in relation to you at this moment. That is why it is so difficult to pin down the meaning of love. I think the best way of describing it is to say that love is really just a *context*, an attitude of heart that allows whatever thoughts, feelings and wishes that there may be, to be what they are. It is like psychological fresh air or a warming fire. It is an underlying attitude that unconditionally supports the life, integrity and growth of other people regardless of whether they agree or disagree with you. This means, I think, that love is an orientation of heart towards the entire world and everything in it. Either you relate to the whole thing, including yourself, with an orientation of love, or you don't love at all. You cannot say "I'll love this but not that", because as soon as you do this you are not loving at all. Instead, you are judging, grading, comparing or imposing your plans. As soon as we try to select who or what we will love, we are immediately, in the very act of selecting, taking an unloving attitude. The whole point about love is that it is unselective; it is accepting and supporting towards everything that exists.

This is extremely difficult to put into words because it is very easy to misunderstand what is meant and, for example, imagine that 'acceptance' means 'approval'. We get so carried away with our own judgements that we can hardly conceive of what it might mean to take a non-judgemental attitude. Mistakenly, we think that to do this would be to approve of everything. But this isn't being non-judgemental, this would be the (foolish) judgement that everything was 'good', which, clearly, is not true.

Those who have been brought up in a loving atmosphere will, without necessarily knowing it, tend to re-create such a supportive atmosphere wherever they go and whoever they are with. Those who have not lived in a loving context will, on the other hand, find it much more difficult to learn what love is because they will not even be able to love themselves. There are, in other words, both virtuous and vicious cycles. However, we can, I think, get a glimpse or be reminded of what love is. When you are with someone who creates a loving atmosphere it is like being reminded of something you had forgotten about rather than like receiving anything new.

The person who lives in an atmosphere of love is the one most able to grow and change, whereas others, living in a non-loving environment, constantly feel moulded, judged, condemned, blamed and unaccepted for what they are. Such people end up not loving themselves and yet they find growth and change very difficult to achieve. One part of the unloved self becomes the internalised judge, who is constantly scolding and complaining. Another part becomes the oppressed under-dog, who is always apologising, promising to be better and try harder, but who, underneath, resents being bullied and resists and sabotages change the whole time.

The more we have lived in a warm, loving atmosphere, the more we will experience our 'voice of conscience' as being sunny, warm and supportive in tone. Whereas if, in our past, there has been a great lack of love, then we will find that our conscience is a bully which condemns, complains, punishes and tortures. The result of this is that we will have a perpetually low opinion of ourselves. We internalise within ourselves the tone of voice that we have most regularly heard.

If we don't value and have respect for ourselves, quite regardless of our successes and failures, then we will find that we are caught in a double-bind. Whenever we try to offer anything to others we will think, "Since I am worthless there is nothing that I can give to others that is worth very much"; and when, on the other hand, people seek to give anything to us we will think, "If this person really knew me, she would never offer me anything at all. Her gifts are fragile and unreliable since they are based on a misunderstanding about who I really am. I don't deserve them."

An atmosphere of love first and foremost helps us to develop a basic respect for ourselves, without which we will find it very difficult to have respect for others. Such an atmosphere creates a sense of space and support. Regardless of any circumstances whatsoever, regardless of whatever you and others are feeling, there is an underlying sense that you and others and the world as a whole are 'O.K.' Not in the sense of being judged and evaluated as O.K., but in that you feel accepted and supported. In such an atmosphere you don't have to put on a show for others, or for yourself. You don't have to try to be someone else; to think or feel anything other than what you do think or feel. And because you are accepted by others as you are, you can start to learn to accept others. Great changes then become possible.

Obviously, in creating such a loving atmosphere, certain types of behaviour, emotions and attitudes are more helpful than others. A capacity to relax, to listen, to empathise, to show your feelings honestly and openly, to stand up for yourself without having to put down others, all help in creating an atmosphere of love. Indeed all the other characteristics that I have been describing in this book help to create and are created by such an atmosphere; and so I would add to the above list the ability to behave responsibly, to be aware, to avoid guilt and useless worry and, not least, the ability to exert control over oneself and to know that this control is not the same thing as repression. These character-istics are, in fact, so intimately interconnected with each other that I have frequently found it almost impossible to talk about any one of them without referring to the others. Each, undoubtedly, is more fully understood as we come to understand all the others.

However, it is important to realise that we cannot wait until we become such ideal paragons of virtue before we start to love or, otherwise, we will wait forever. To repeat what I said at the beginning of the book, these qualities are ideals to aim at and, by their nature, we never finally reach or realise them. We can move towards them without it even making sense to talk of our 'getting there'.

And so I have to accept that, like everyone else, I will always be liable to useless tension, ineffective listening, poor empathy and dishonest and manipulative ways. I will at times remain irresponsible, half asleep, and I will both repress and indulge emotions. Moreover I will feel guilty and worry uselessly from time to time. We *can* significantly reduce all these self-defeating behaviours, but it is a most obsessive affectation to think or hope that we can ever get rid of them altogether. Understanding these basic virtues, (and people have understood them for thousands of years!) is far easier than actually living up to them.

Thus, to repeat, we must all gently nudge ourselves towards creating a loving atmosphere while we are still frogs, as it were, because if we wait until we become 'whiter-than-white' we will wait forever. It is just as well that the loving attitude involves a willingness to forgive, and to encourage and see the good in people. Because there will be endless occasions where we will need to forgive both ourselves and others as we, over and over again, witness the hurt and harm that we inflict on others and they throw back at us. There is not even any justice in these exchanges of aggression and violence. At any one time, some people will rightly or wrongly, feel that they have more reason to nurse grievances and hurts than others. But it will be no good if we say, "I will forgive all the hurts and injustices you have inflicted on me as long as I can wrong you back just as much". This is the revenge mentality, and there is never agreement about the 'fair' allocation of punishment, which in any case does no one any good. With a capacity to empathise with others we can begin to understand why they behave towards us in the way they do, and this can help us to forgive. But it won't make us like hurt and aggression any the more!

There is, though, at least some reassurance to be gained if we remember that our capacity, potential and wish to love and be loved is very great. Certainly there is far more potential to love than we generally manage to express. If love was measured in terms of good *intentions* then it would be a very loving world indeed! Underneath all the fear, posturing, manouvering and self-obsession we tend to want to unfold and to meet the unfolded 'other' in a way that is mutually supportive and caring, and that wants and seeks for the best in other people. Of course, our intentions are often a long way behind our *achievements; and our ability to express* love is often very poor. Intentions, though, if by no means 'satisfactory' on their own, are at least a step in the right direction!

A final point. Love does not provide safety, security and certainty about the future. Rather, it gives us the strength and courage to face the fact that the future is unknown, uncertain and involves risks. When you are loved you are

not cocooned against the knocks and bumps of living, rather
you are assisted in standing, ultimately, on your own two
feet and empowered with the confidence and courage to
trust that you will, somehow, cope with, learn from and
even enjoy whatever mysteries there are lying around the
next corner. Love, in other words, is not a defence against
life-seen-as-a-threat. It is not a place of refuge that we can
use when we are running away from life. Instead, it gives us
the strength to commit ourselves wholeheartedly in a life
that in its essence consists of perpetual change and which at
bottom remains a mystery to us; something that we can
never altogether understand. In giving us this strength, love
inevitably helps us to see what it really means to be a strong
person. Many of us, (especially men!), have a completely
inaccurate vision of what it is to be strong. The male
stereotype, for example, is that of the person with somewhat
gritted teeth, a 'tough' expression on his face, tensed up
muscles ready for a fight, an aggressive, ruthless manner, a
certain insensitivity to others and lack of willingness to get
too close to people, and an ability to repress feelings, or,
preferably, to avoid even having many feelings at all. If I was
stronger myself I could weep at the sight of so many boys
who, when learning to be 'real men', take on all these
'tough', 'strong' styles of behaviour. The truth is that all
these attitudes and behaviours are the very opposite of
strength and life. They are in fact weakness and the death of
sensibility. Anyone who goes around with a tough, hard,
shell of a face is in fact afraid and hiding inside without even
realising it. Would you walk through a field of daisies with
a 'tough guy' expression on your face, fists clenched and
biceps flexing? Of course not. And why? Because there is no
perceived threat. You would look ridiculous trying to look
tough when confronted with only flowers, which is why the
'tough' guy tends to avoid being in such nurturing
environments. He doesn't know what to do with them.

And so it is that the constant expression of toughness in
reality masks an underlying fear of attack. A fear that cannot
be brought into awareness because (supposedly) it is
weakness to admit and show that you are afraid.

With real strength we can face and admit to our fears, and
the greatest experts in, for example, the martial arts know

this. The fighter who stands like a fortress of stone, throwing stiff punches like a battering ram has no chance against the boxer who moves like a willow. And few boxers would last long against the real dancers of the Eastern martial arts, who are intimately aware of their feelings and bodies and whose movements are more like that of water than stone. Such people are really strong because they have discovered the profound truth that strength comes from outside us, or, rather, that the boundaries between self and non-self are a convention required by the mind and not an absolute required by existence. Such a fighter thus discovers connectedness with others so that although he is more capable of inflicting great physical damage on others he seeks most of all to avoid doing so. His greatest victory comes in being able to defuse potentially violent situations by peaceful means. Hence the most proficient fighters in the martial arts have never fought at all except in practice. They may start off with the thought that by learning such a skill they will become better than others and able to dominate others. But they end up in learning what it is to love and to experience their connectedness with everyone and everything around them. The thought of striking another then becomes as abhorrent as it would be to strike a blow to their own body. Such awareness does not make them better people; it simply shows that they have discovered the truth that all schemes for domination and perceptions of separation are illusions.

Chapter Seven. Love

Summary:

Difficulty of the subject. Many possible meanings when people say "I love you". Love not the same as agreeing with people. Agreements needed in order to live with people. Love not the same as judging, evaluating, grading. Love connected with giving; but not about being exploited and being a doormat. The need to stand up for yourself in order to gain respect. Giving does not mean ignoring your own wishes. Giving *or* getting? – a false choice. The selfish think that getting is better than giving. The puritanical think that giving is better than getting. Giving in order to get is simply investment. Phony human relations courses that are about investment. Getting is O.K. too. How can you give if people won't receive? Our own well-being ultimately not at odds with that of others. Sick versions of God; the all-judging policeman/accountant; based on fear and lack of love. Can we love the person even if we don't like some of their behaviour? Love not conditional on behaviour. Love: Not blind to evil but does not condemn the person. Does not manipulate the person. Seeks out the best in people. Compassionate, mending and healing. Respects the right of others to choose for themselves. Does not 'mould' people. Doesn't involve 'putting on a show'. Doesn't mean that we are free of conflict and confusion. Not the same as intimacy. Not about needing particular people. Not about owning and clinging, which leads to suffocation. Between adult and child *is* based on dependence. The you-and-me-against-the-world syndrome. Romantic infatuation. The market-place approach. Do we know how to love? Love not any particular emotion; a 'context' – like fresh air. Love involves acceptance and unconditional support. Love is an attitude towards the entire world; either we love it all or we don't really know love. Vicious and virtuous cycles. The 'internalised judge', 'underdog' and 'saboteur'. The double-bind of low self-esteem; if others love you, you think it is based on illusion, and if you love you consider it worthless because you see yourself as worthless. Certain behaviours help to create a loving atmosphere – the entire book explores these. Ideals cannot be finally achieved. Forgiveness of ourselves and others needed. Forgiveness not according to a sense of justice, or otherwise it is a revenge mentality. Love does not involve safety, serenity and certainty about the future. Love gives us courage to face uncertainty; not a place where we can hide away. Love teaches us the truth about what it is to be strong.

Questions and Exercises:

1. Think about the last time you said "I love you". Did you mean it when you said it? What else might you have meant? Do you think others meant it when they said it to you?

2. Can you genuinely love people even when you don't agree with them? Will you give others permission to be themselves regardless of whether or not you like it?

3. When you think you love someone, how far are you actually judging, evaluating, grading them?

4. Can you give to other people without being used as a doormat?

5. Can you show others that you are going to stand up for yourself and at the same time show that you love them?

6. Can you love yourself and forgive yourself for all your foolish ways? Right now, and over and over again? Remember, until you can love yourself and respect yourself you are going to find it extremely difficult to love others.

7. Can you give time, attention or whatever to others, without expecting anything in return?

8. Can you receive gifts from others without assuming that you owe the other person anything at all? Don't you think that you deserve good things – just because you are a living person?

9. Notice the pleasure you get when you give things. But notice also how you spoil it for yourself if you give *in order to feel* this pleasure.

8. Psychology and Religion

Religion, as understood by most people, (clergy, laypeople and most psychologists), has nothing to do with psychology. It is all about having a comprehensive belief system that gives you answers to the most profound questions we can ask; like, "What is the purpose of life?" "Where did the universe come from and where is it going?" and "How do I fit into the overall scheme of things?" Each of the various religious traditions, in the eyes of most people, will provide you with a set of 'facts' about the world, people and the universe as a whole. Also, you are provided with a set of instructions about what we ought to do and a code of values about what is important, and what is right and wrong. This is all very cosy and reassuring to us when, as is so often the case, we don't want to face the extent to which we *don't know* the answers to such fundamental questions.

Religion seen as a provider of facts has run into a great deal of difficulty, particularly in the West, in the past few centuries because we have, rightly I think, become much more fussy about wanting 'evidence' for any so-called facts that there may be about the world. In the Middle Ages, and earlier, it was possible to sit around and dream up any number of ideas and, if you had enough authority or could pretend that you were interpreting an old and revered book, you could get others to believe that your dreams and fancies were the truth. You could even convince yourself that this was so, and anyone asking for evidence could be in serious trouble. The beliefs that people had were determined by what the authorities thought and said and, even more important, by what was to be found in old revered books like, for example, the Holy Bible. You were not expected to question such beliefs and think independently for yourself. To ask for evidence and coherent reasoning was considered heresy.

Nowadays, of course, we tend to be much more careful about wanting to check whether there really is good evidence for any 'wise person's' claims, and we like to look inside ourselves to see if the claims square with our own experience. We still, naturally, have authority figures, specialists and experts, but however famous and brilliant the authority may be, we always assume that his arguments and evidence can and should be examined and questioned by others. We have abandoned the notion that any one person or group of persons is infallible such that their words must be accepted without question. This is, I think, one of the greatest and most precious achievements of our culture and I hope that we never allow ourselves, through carelessness or intimidation, to let go of it. There are, of course, just a few cults or sects where criticism, questioning and independence of thought are not encouraged; but they are, by and large, the exception rather than the rule in the West. This is not to say that the quality of people's independent thinking and questioning is all that it might be. Far from it! Most people remain remarkably sluggish about examining old habits and ideas, and tend to accept whatever notions are handed out to them with very little questioning and thought. But at least the *principle* of wanting evidence and argument is well established, even though many are prepared to let others do the work that is involved.

The results of such diligent checking for facts show that the evidence for what actually occurred when someone called Jesus walked the face of the Earth is extremely fragmented and limited. We have few old manuscripts, no one seems to have written anything down about Christ during his lifetime, documents are contradictory and written more as poetry and metaphor than factual history. Different authors were involved whose identity is often unclear; and amendments and changes in text were made over the intervening centuries. The evidence is so limited that we cannot actually *reconstruct* a picture of what happened at all. There is scarcely anything that we can say about the historical Jesus that we can be certain is actually the truth. No court of law, no scientist, no biographer, no historian taking an open-minded look at the evidence could come to any other conclusion, in my view, than that they don't really know what happened in the Middle East 2,000 years ago to someone who might have been called Jesus. And so it is that in schools in England, when Christianity is taught, the various traditional stories are told but teachers often veer away in embarrassment on the question of whether or not they are actually true. Most people sense or know that the evidence is hopelessly flimsy, but there remains a sort of genteel reluctance to say so too often or too explicitly. Without these nice old stories, many people imagine, what would happen to the moral basis of society? Therefore, it is thought, it is best not to look too carefully. We must try to keep the rickety edifice called Christianity going because we don't imagine that we can find anything to replace it. Such reserve, I suggest, has been a disaster for religion and for morals in this country. It has meant that people now seem to have very little idea of what religion at its best can be all about, and our moral code has been left to rest on the feeble foundations of what are often shallow and inadequate stories that do not even impress a ten year old.

On the other hand, the evidence for the historical Buddha and most of the other great religious teachers is often just as inadequate. We have very little solid information about the most 'well-known' religious teachers. Most of them have been dead for over a thousand years and everything that they ever may have said has been passed on to us by writers who have inevitably coloured everything they 'report' with their own interpretations and biases and understandings of the teaching. It is as though every teaching in every religious tradition has been handed down to us as a result of a centuries-old process of 'Chinese Whispers'. In this parlour game a message is passed around a circle of a dozen or more people, each whispering it on to the next, and the person who originally sent it marvels at the garbled form that comes back to him after its journey around the group. How much more interpretation and distortion is there likely to be when the messages involved are much more ancient and, by their nature, enigmatic and wide open to various ways of being understood?

For years I was tempted to conclude that because the

historical picture they gave was so shaky and unreliable, the only thing worth doing with religious teachings was to scrap them. This, though, I suggest, is a mistake. The value of looking at various religious teachings comes not from what factual claims they make about the world, but rather from what they *suggest* about how to live that seems useful and usable to us now. In other words, we can consider the (would-be) 'wise' words of some authority and each decide for ourselves whether or not what is being said is valuable and worthwhile. We each of us make up our own minds as to whether or not we will add our vote to the proposal that someone is an authority worth following. And if you look for yourselves and think for yourselves you will, I think, find that some ancient teachers say things that strike you as profoundly insightful and supportive; while others come out with observations that are banal, wrong-headed, confused, insane, irrelevant, immature or whatever. Indeed, a person might say something worth quoting for a thousand years and then, only minutes later, make a perfectly fatuous or foolish observation that we would be wise to ignore. No one, in my experience, has cornered the market on Wisdom, and no one, let me repeat, is infallible. Even the greatest sages make foolish and mistaken remarks and, come to think of it, it would be quite salutory to compile a book that listed some of the stupidest remarks made by the greatest teachers! It would encourage us all to keep on our toes and never read or listen uncritically.

But what about the historical picture? What actually did happen in Israel, or India, or China two, three, or four thousand years ago? The truth is that our knowledge of such ancient history is always likely to remain very scanty; it may be disappointing, that our curiosity will never finally be satisfied, but it is not crucial to the understanding of religion and morality. What really matters is whether the remnants of old teachings that we have are alive and valuable to us here and now. What if some wit and genius several centuries ago re-wrote the teachings of a more ancient master and managed to do this without our knowing? This clearly prevents us from having the earlier version, it is somewhat unethical, it is particularly irresponsible behaviour for any historian, but it might also be that the re-written version is

far more profound and valuable to us than the original
would have been. A contemporary writer, Carlos Castaneda,
wrote of a 'living' American Indian guru called Don Juan
whose teachings Castaneda claimed to have studieed at the
feet of this Indian master. He even got a Phd. degree from
the University of California for his work of social anthropology, and his publishers still treat it as a factual work.
Critics, on the other hand, have argued that the evidence
points to Don Juan being a fictional character created from
Castaneda's own mind! If this is so then certainly the
University of California's Department of Anthropology has
cause for concern, but the teaching itself stands or falls on its
own merits. If it is fiction it simply means that the
spiritual/moral teacher is Castaneda rather than Don Juan.
The evidence does seem to me to be that Castaneda is
mimicking the Guru/Trickster tradition of some American
Indian tribes – with great success! Of the teaching itself, it is,
in my opinion, good in parts.

What has any of this got to do with psychology? Superfic-
ially there may be no connection at all, but increasingly
psychologists are coming to take an interest in the connections between what they are doing and what religion of
whatever tradition might be about. This has arisen as a result
of the work of people like, for example, Assagioli, Jung,
Maslow, Fromm and Rogers. What these researchers have in
common is that they have not simply considered what it
might mean to be living below one's potential, or to be below
'normal', but rather they have turned the question around
and asked what would it be like to be using one's potential
to the full; to be functioning more effectively than the norm?
This leads on to asking what is 'wisdom'? and what is
'maturity'? and, before long, you find that you are on the
same quest as religious seekers; the truest of who have
always been asking precisely these questions.

Now, of course, questions like "what is wisdom?" and
"what is maturity?" are not the sort for which you can find
neat easy answers. They cannot be answered once and for
all. However, they are, surely, important questions to ask,
and the process of *trying* to answer them can be extremely
valuable and worthwhile. My own view is that the more you
push deeply into these questions, the more you find out that

you already know far more about them than you might have thought. When we recognise and appreciate people with truly exceptional talents and qualities it is, I think, because we, too, have these qualities in some smaller way latent within ourselves. If this were not so, I suggest, we would be much less likely to see and recognise the qualities at all. To illustrate this, there is, for example, the old saying about the saint and the pickpocket: A person who was *nothing but* a pickpocket, it is suggested, would only see a saint's pockets and not the saint. In fact the criminal can recognise the qualities of a 'saintly' person, and respect them, because deep down inside himself he knows that these are desirable qualities. He 'already knows'. What is more, the mature and wise person knows that others already have maturity and wisdom latent within them. I was recently watching a film based on the life of Mahatma Gandhi which brought this point out. Gandhi's magnificent achievement, the film suggested, was not simply the result of what he personally did. After all, what can one single person achieve? The magnificence lay in his capacity to assist millions of others to get a glimpse of their own extraordinary powers and to use this. What Gandhi did was to get people to see that they, too, could achieve the impossible, could rise above their human weaknesses at least some of the time. Ordinary people could discover their own wisdom and maturity, and act on it with great courage.

The magnificence was also laced, perhaps inevitably, with tragedy. As well as discovering the insight that we are all capable of, we also saw the great folly and destructiveness, fear and delusion that we succumb to. The murderer recognises wisdom because he has these qualities latent within himself. The wise person, similarly, recognises and knows the murderer, because we all of us have those capacities for destruction latent, and not so latent, within us.

I have discussed this subject of wisdom and maturity with many adult education groups in the last few years and, rather than pretend to be able to give answers, I have suggested that we all work out for ourselves together what these qualities might be. There has been an extraordinary amount of agreement about this; indeed many of the ideas in this book have been clarified as a result of such group discussion. For example, people will be quick to suggest that the wise person is not someone who gets up on a soapbox and pretends to know everything, but rather is someone who is honest enough to know that she doesn't know. And so it is that, in courses on comparative religion, the monks, priests and teachers who impress groups the most are the ones who do not pretend to have all the answers, and who do not push dogma at all.

Certainly, the clergy who attract me the most are the ones who hardly seem to care whether you are a Buddhist, or Anglican, or Humanist, or Hindu, or Catholic, or whatever. All the ritual and paraphernalia of these traditions is seen by the people who 'really know' to be merely devices that point and help you to something beyond ritual and belief. The beliefs and rituals are merely means to an end; they are not ends in themselves. And so if you cling to the beliefs and ritual it is as though you were walking around with a signpost under your arm, pretending that you have reached your destination. Or, to put it another way, clinging to belief is like hanging on to a set of tools and pretending that you had produced a beautiful piece of craftsmanship.

The people who, I suggest, really know about religion, (they are a small minority and always have been), know that it doesn't matter which *means* you use to achieve this particular end. You may travel on a Buddhist Road, or Hindu, or Humanist or whatever. What counts is whether or not you travel anywhere worthwhile on these roads; whether you get anywhere. People who have made some progress on a journey don't worry which bus they travelled on; but the zealots, and dogmatists and fools are busy polishing the vehicle and arguing that theirs is the shiniest and best, and not noticing that it is going nowhere for them.

Thus it is that the people who seem most to understand what religion is don't really care very much about belief. I have come to the conclusion that 'belief' has got little to do with understanding the heart of religion; what really matters is how you *experience* the world and how you *behave* in it.

Don't we already know in our hearts that this is the truth? Suppose you visualise in your minds a 'great' theologian and scholar. He has read thousands of books about religion. Perhaps he has also been in monasteries for years. He can tell you who said what in different parts of the world over the last 4,000 years. He is familiar with all the great texts. But so what? The test as to whether or not all this knowledge and belief is of any value and importance comes when we see whether or not he puts any of it to actual use in his everyday life. If it doesn't make any difference to the way he experiences the world and behaves in it then surely all his knowledge is worthless? If the knowledge has influenced behaviour and attitudes, then there is some point in having it and taking it seriously. But if it has not then can we say that this is a religious person? Can we say that this person really knows anything about religion? I think not, and quite possibly the most unskilled and ignorant labourer could, depending on his actions and attitudes to life, be seen as far more religious than the scholar.

The acid test then, the road to the heart of religion, wisdom and maturity, I suggest, is not to be found in the information that we have, but rather in what we do with it. Ultimately what matters is what we do and how we relate to the world. Information is only of use if it is actually used. The adult education groups that I have been involved with have sometimes developed quite an acute sense of this. To begin with they have paid attention to the information, instruction, rules and codes when listening to religious teachers. But then they have started to realise that the real test is how the monk or teacher actually lives. Have the beliefs made any practical difference that seems worthwhile? And so they start to pay more attention to the way a visitor enters the room, the way he or she relates to other people, the way any beliefs have made a difference in practice.

Given that experience and behaviour, rather than belief, is the key it becomes important to find out what such experience and behaviour is that might be called 'religious'. We also need to see how the experience and behaviour interconnect. I want to begin, though, with the matter of religious experience. What is this? What are (at least some of) its features?

Being at One with the world

The religious person has a capacity to feel herself to be a part of the world, and not separate from and at odds with it. In this way, she has a deeper understanding of who she is than most of us. (And so, for example, see Chapter five on "Personal Identity", which shows how closely psychology and religion can move together). The secular view is to see ourselves as separate from, and in conflict with the rest of the world. We each try to 'triumph' over Nature and score 'victories' over others, as though these were in opposition to us. The more things we can get for ourselves, the more achievements and victories that are 'ours', the more we think we have become. As I have said before, the motto becomes, "I have, I triumph, I win, therefore I exist."

The truth is that we cannot triumph over anything, nor can we be defeated by anything, because we are not at odds with it. The leaf does not triumph over the tree; it is a part of what the tree is doing. The person doesn't triumph over the world; she is part of what the world is doing.

The religious person has a capacity at least to get a glimpse of the world as one interconnected totality. It is one great symphony, one great harmony, in the sense that everything is intimately connected with and dependent on everything else. There is no separation. The delusion of separation arises because, in order for our minds to be able to make sense of the world, we have to imagine it divided up into 'things', objects and events. We simply cannot deal with it in any other way. The mind is not big enough to be able to apprehend the world as one undivided totality, and so it has to subdivide and subdivide in order to be able to understand it one small piece at a time. It can then move on slowly seeing connections between pieces, one connection at a time.

Ultimately, all the separations we make of so-called different objects are arbitrary, in the sense that they have got much more to do with the way the mind is structured than the way the world is. With its limited memory and limited powers of reasoning and apprehension, the mind must say "Here are objects, here are events, this has influenced that, here is you, this is me", and so on. The young child does not have the capacity or experience to grasp large interrelated systems or entities like cities or institutions or ideologies. Similarly, at some stage, our own mental capacity fails to grasp an interrelated totality. And so we certainly fail to grasp the totality of the 'One-ness' of the universe. Perhaps some super-mind could see and really understand this as one whole interrelated entity in the way that a really good mechanic might apprehend an engine. But we humans cannot. The religious person might *sense* an interconnectedness, but it is not something he can understand and get on top of in any intellectual sense.

What he can do, though, is to watch all the so-called objects and circumstances of life go by, without either getting attached to them or running away from them. In this way he can start to gain a perspective that goes beyond ego while at the same time being a full participant. As a result of this he can begin to gain a sense of the overall process of existence and thus see that objects are more accurately events that last a little longer than is considered 'normal'. None of these can exist or be understood in isolation from everything else. With this kind of perception, a person can begin to grasp that the emotions, ideas and wishes that he experiences are, in an important sense, no more nor less 'his' than sunshine, or the birds flying by, or the sound of the radio. It all simply arises and passes away. It is not strictly gone because it is not strictly a separate 'thing' at all. It has only gone in the sense that we are no longer apprehending it.

The religious person has a sense of interrelatedness, or one-ness; but any attempt to describe this must ultimately fall short, because we are trying to apprehend something that the mind cannot really apprehend at all. We can merely sense unity as that which lies beyond our mental grasp. It is as though there was something at the very edge of our visual field of perception, such that we could know that there was something there, but not know what it was. In visual perception, of course, we can turn our head and look. In mental apprehension of that which is too large for the mind to grasp, there is nothing we can do except remain with the sense of vastness, space, unity and mystery.

With a secular apprehension, we move with, explore and deal with that which we know, with what we can understand and grasp with our minds. With a religious apprehension, on the other hand, we see 'what we know' in the context of 'that which we don't know'; of what we don't grasp; of that which lies beyond us. This results in a fairly predictable pattern of emotional response. For example, a sense of awe, of humility, of reverence for the whole of life in its mystery, a willingness to accept what is; but also a sense of very great strength and trust.

If you see yourself as separate from and at odds with the world then any strength you think you may have seems fragile, insecure, temporary, and this sense of separation is the essence of the non-religious apprehension of the world. (Indeed, the Latin root of the word religion is, I am told, *religio*, which means 'to re-connect'. In other words with religion we are re-connected with the rest of the world around us, or more accurately, we discover that our sense of being separate was a delusion). The secular person, feeling ultimately separate from and at odds with everything around him, imagines that he is besieged by the rest of the world. When you are in such a mood, for how long can you hold out? For how long can you find allies, supplies, support and strength from within yourself? Ultimately, you sense, you will lose. The world will engulf you. Death will overtake you. The sense of hollowness inside seems a threat to your survival. You are like a brittle shell that can be broken. All that you have can be lost. You have to be armed and armoured because basically you fear and mistrust all that is around you.

On the other hand, if you don't see yourself as separate from the world then you can sense that the whole of the world is supporting you. You are a part of what it is doing. Instead of seeing yourself as a fortress, you can see yourself as more like a helpless baby. Without all your life-support systems, all of which lie ultimately beyond your control, you would not survive for one second. It is as though you were utterly dependent on your umbilical cord to the world. You have to let go and trust, because there is only pain and suffering if you try to resist and see yourself as separate.

This is why paying attention to breathing has so often been considered crucial in religion and, for that matter, in psychology. If you can trust, you will be able to breathe out fully and relax, because you will trust that the next breath will come and that, in the meantime, you don't have to be on your guard. Moreover, if you can trust and let go, you can find that this great mystery that lies beyond you, the emptiness that lies within you, is a source of considerable strength and support. It is from the 'nothingness' that everything that supports us comes. The breath comes. the thought comes. The feelings come. The wishes come. All this something comes from nowhere, as it were.

The religious person, to put it another way, is not so much living his life, ploughing his way through it, but is, rather, letting it live through him. In a secular mood we imagine that we have to go after life; pin it down; push our way through, like a ship pushing its way through a resisting ocean. In a spiritual mood, we see that the ship is not pushing through a resisting sea; it is simply one whole process. The water moves out of the way, the air feeds the engines helping the oil to burn, everything gets on with being itself, and can do so only with the support and co-operation of all that lies beyond it. And so it is that we can realise that we don't have to chase life, pin it down or corner it. Life is constantly flowing through us from that mystery that is beyond us. Thoughts, feelings, wishes and actions just come. Who we are and what lies beyond us remains, at bottom, a mystery and yet, paradoxically, by trusting this unknown and going with it we find that we can cope, and that there is always support.

Some people call this Nothing, this mystery, this unknown, 'God', and do not pretend that they have any understanding of this. I don't personally find the word useful at all, because it is so associated with big father-figures, neat answers and dogma – the very antithesis of spirituality. Similarly, 'prayer' is a word that I find full of negative associations. If it is all about asking for special favours and special treatment, so that you can score victories over others in your battle with the world, then it is immature, pathetic, and rests on the illusion of a separate self. If, on the other hand, it is all about being still, centering yourself, sensing your connectedness with everything and trusting that you will find the strength and insight to do the next thing to be done, then it makes far more sense. Words like 'God' and 'prayer' are, it seems, sometimes used in ways that are powerful and significant. More often, though, they are not, and the actual meaning of spirituality is thus often completely lost within the established (so-called) religious institutions and traditions. Religion then becomes, undoubtedly, an opiate for the people, which, although helping to create a quiet life, takes people still further away from realising their full potential.

It is very interesting to explore the different ways in which the great mythical stories of Christianity (and other religious traditions) can be, and have been, variously interpreted. Some interpretations are valuable and important, alive and life-making. Others reflect fear, ignorance and dogma, and dull people's awareness and capacity to act responsibly. For example, the myth of the devil as a rebellious angel thrown out from Heaven by God can be seen in (at least) two ways. One is that of seeing God as the mafia-style Godfather who has a bit of trouble with a rebellious henchman and shows him that He is still Boss. Such a father we will fear. The rebellious devil gets attacked by God, but manages to escape. God is not defeated by him but neither does He manage to wipe him out.

The moral of such a story is clear. Keep in line with the Godfather or else He will personally give you a rough time. On the other hand, move too far away from Him and He will lose His influence over you, but you will then come under a new tyranny, that of the devil. God is thus a well-meaning tyrant who gives you a safe, dull, time but says that it is in your best long-term interests. The devil is a cunning tyrant who will tempt you away with offers of fun and excitement, but who will make you suffer in the long run. (Fun and excitement, the puritan has long thought, are bad and people must therefore *pay* for them in the end!)

Another possible interpretation of this myth is quite different. This involves saying that the devil was an angel who imagined that he could be separate from and apart from the rest of life. The devil imagined that he could be at odds with the world, could defy it and conquer it, without needing it and being dependent on it. The suffering that arises from such an attitude is not any kind of retribution from a punishing Godfather, but, rather it is an immediate and inevitable consequence of self-created delusion.

It is the suffering, for example, that would occur if a baby in the womb decided that it had to find itself a safe and secure place of protection and source of supply, as a result of failing to realise that all this was already available and being dealt with for it. In the same way, the minute we forget that we are *already* firmly supported by, and grounded in, the earth and the air, we suffer. We start to imagine that we must carve a special protected place for ourselves where we will be safe and secure, and no longer threatened by everything around us; and we set off and turn our life's work into that of finding such a place. Immediately, though, there is pain, because our fundamental attitude is now that we are not safe and not supported. We start to look for a real home, all the time forgetting that the entire world is our home already, and that all that happens within it is a gift rather than a snag. 'Enlightenment', therefore, is not about getting to a special place, or becoming a special person with extra-ordinary powers and insights; it is all about knowing that wherever you are and whatever you are doing and thinking is already very special, and there is nowhere else more wonderful to go to or to be. There is nowhere special or safe to go to because you have already arrived. But it can take people years, sometimes, to realise this. Some people put an enormous amount of time and energy into following a 'spiritual path'. They want to discover the 'philosopher's stone', the crock of gold at the end of the rainbow, the magic box with the secret scrolls giving the most deep and 'inner' wisdom of the ages. They want to become exceptional, super people, who can walk on water, lie on beds of nails, deal with great stresses with a powerful sense of calm and competence. They are in search of the miraculous.

You can spend you entire life in search of the miraculous, and there are any number of rituals, customs, practices, theories and other devices to keep you amused while you are on this (so-called) trail. There are various tests you can give yourself to measure how advanced you are, how far along the trail you are. It is a very time-consuming game. 'Special' people are sought after, the gurus or great teachers, who, it is considered, have the secret knowledge and who have 'arrived'. They are enlightened, they know the Truth, they are different from the rest of us.

It may be that some of us have to play the game of searching for the miraculous; searching for special powers and insights. But it really is rather like the party game in which the prize is stuck to your own back and is already yours. The dif-

ference between the enlightened and the un-enlightened
person, it has been suggested, is that un-enlightened people
think that there is such a thing as enlightenment, (special
places, special powers, silver boxes with scrolls of the 'inner
knowledge'). Enlightened people, on the other hand, know
that there is no such thing. The 'ordinary', for the person
who 'knows', is miracle enough. We are all miraculous,
special, supported, connected to everything else already.

Sometimes, I think, the very searching for the miraculous
takes us further away from realising it. Because, for as long
as we are searching, we are taking the view that the place we
are at right now is *not it*. Our present surroundings, friends,
thoughts, feelings and actions are not good enough. We
want something better. With the enlightened person, on the
other hand, everything here now is miraculous, fine, 'good
enough', a gift to be learned from and used. The enlightened, thus, seeks to make changes (the very essence of being
alive) while at the same time being fully in love with the way
everything is right now.

There is a wonderful old story that makes this point about
'enlightenment' very well. It also underlines the importance
of behaviour as opposed to belief. This is the story of the Sufi
master who was also a cobbler. I can't remember where I first
came across this story, but this hardly matters. The story
would be neither more nor less important if (Castaneda-
fashion!) I had just invented it myself.

First some background. The Sufis are, as it were, the
mystical wing, or sect, in Islam. In other words, they actually
know what religion is all about as a spiritual matter rather
than preoccupying themselves with dead ritual, dogma, and
belief. Sufi teachers are renowned for their 'low profile'
existence. They hide themselves away and get on with living
in the community rather than surrounding themselves with
accolytes, or sitting on pedestals wearing tall hats. There was
once, we are told, a disciple of Sufism who was keen to trace
a particular master considered to be exceptionally learned
and wise in the ways of Sufism. He, more than anyone else
alive, it was thought, knew of the wise teachings that had
been handed down from the Great Old Masters from
thousands of years ago. "If I could only get this man to train
me", the disciple thought, "I would really be saved; I would

really learn the teachings, I would really be able to get close to understanding the sacred texts and ancient rituals."

Suffice it to say that, after much searching, the disciple found his teacher hiding away in some remote village and living a very ordinary sort of existence on the surface. In order not to attract too much attention, it seemed, the Great Master passed himself off as a cobbler.

"I will teach you the ways of the Sufis," the disciple was told, "but first I want you to work with me in this trade. As you can see, I make and repair the shoes for people hereabouts. If you are to be useful to me, and to them, you will need to learn how to fix and make shoes. I will teach you how, but don't, in the meantime, keep on at me about the teachings of the Great Masters. All that will come in its time, but not if you keep pestering me about it."

And so it was that the disciple took up the craft of shoe-repair, and wondered to himself just how long he would have to wait before the Master took him into his own private chambers to show him the incense, the scrolls, the robes, the incantations and all the rest. Shoe-repair might be needed as a starting place on the training, the Master, surely knew best. But when would they really get started with the more obviously spiritual parts of the training?

Very occasionally the disciple would ask the Master, "will it be soon before we begin the teachings?" but always he would reply:

"You are doing quite well, please show patience, because these things cannot be rushed."

Well, five, ten, twelve, twenty or however many years went by. The disciple became skilled in his trade, was seen by all the villagers as a cobbler rather than a disciple of Sufism, and was a respected member and much loved part of his community. One morning, the Sufi master came to his disciple and said. "This is just another day and yet it is also a very special day. For I want to tell you that I consider that at last your training is complete. You are wise in the ways of the Sufis. There is nothing else that I can teach you."

The disciple paused, there had been no inner sanctum, no rituals, no scrolls and all the rest. And yet, quietly, it dawned on him as he listened to his master, that yes, he had learned. He now knew what those masters had been trying to pass on. He was 'enlightened' into the secret teachings of Sufism.

What are we to make of this? Are we to suppose that the Sufi master was an imposter, and the disciple a deluded fool? Some would say that this was not Sufism that the disciple had learned, but rather the trade of shoe repair. Scholars of Sufism might say that the story was amusing but irrelevant to the teachings that they had spent years studying. I am convinced that this is one of the most important stories I have come across. The disciple, the story suggests, had learned about religion from the behaviour of the 'Sufi master' rather than from ceremony and belief. The heart of religion, in other words, is to be found in the way we experience and behave in the world, and the Master has taught by example rather than by preaching. The disciple has thus learnt what the essence of Sufism is all about; he has also, in the process, learnt the essence of Buddhism, Christianity and all the rest. On the surface, and particularly in terms of belief and ceremonial, these major religions are very different, but, I suggest, that which is most important and valuable about them is common to them all. However, they are all, unfortunately but inevitably, encrusted with a great deal of ritual and belief which might once have pointed people towards something alive and important but which has died in the hearts of people who failed to grasp its purpose. So much of the incantation and ceremonial of all the major religions, is the empty and worthless incantation of a congregation which has missed the whole point of the exercise.

I must say that I am very attracted to the methods of the cobbler/Sufi master, and there are stories within the other traditions which make the same point. For example, within Buddhism there are various accounts of Buddhist teachers who decide that one of the kitchen porters in the monastery knows more about the teaching than any of the monks who have been studying the texts and following the practices. Certainly Buddhism, more than Christianity, seems to be a tradition that seeks to throw people from attachment to any tradition, such that people who really understand Buddhism are least interested in calling themselves Buddhists. It is always the ignorant disciple who squabbles with

others the most about whether or not their particular creed
is the 'right' one. Can you, for example, imagine Christ and
Buddha engaging in doctrinal disputes or attacking each
other? The more attractive a personality of Christ and
Buddha we create in our minds, the less likely it is that we
can imagine them being anything other than at one with
each other. To repeat, then, it is the experience and
behaviour that counts, and not the doctrine. A person is
religious when she is re-connected to the world, in the sense
of realising that she had never been, and could never be,
separate. But what other features of religious experience are
worth exploring? Let us look at a few more.

Efforts, Obstacles and Conflict

When we see ourselves as separate from the world, we
imagine that there are many battles to be won, and that our
lives consist of constant conflict, with lots of effort needed to
overcome the obstacles thrown up by the world. We are all
familiar with this way of experiencing life.

With a religious, or spiritual, apprehension we don't have
to see things like this. There is no effort, there are no
obstacles, but simply 'that which is involved in doing what
I want to do'. Effort and obstacles only exist for you when
you start to judge that some circumstances in the world
'shouldn't' be as they are. For example: Suppose you had
chosen to build a house at the top of a hill. Suppose the only
way to get the bricks up to the top was to push them up in
a wheelbarrow. We could easily imagine, on our tenth trip,
that the hill was an obstacle and was trying to stop us getting
the job done. But the hill is not an obstacle. It is simply a hill;
and pushing a heavy load up it would simply be the consequence of choosing to build the house on it.

In the same way, with this example, we might say that we
needed to put in lots of 'effort' to get the job done. In one
sense we do need effort. If effort is defined as heavy
breathing, sweating, rapid heart-beat, careful attention to
the job, the tensing up of particular muscles, then clearly we
do need to make plenty of effort. But it doesn't need to be
hard work to make this 'effort'; it can be effortless! The word
effort is closely associated with notions like, "I don't really

want to do this", "I wish it was easier", "I don't like this", "It shouldn't be like this", and so on. None of these notions are necessary or helpful, and, if we can drop them, sweating, muscle tension, mental concentration and all the rest no longer seem like effort and hills no longer seem like obstacles. They are simply the consequences of our choosing what we want to do, and it really is rather stupid to choose a course of action without also choosing the inevitable consequences of this. It is, indeed, irresponsible.

'Effort' is only involved in doing something when a part of us doesn't really want to do it, or where we don't like certain aspects of what we are doing. The effortfulness in other words, comes not from the world itself but from our attitudes towards it! Rather than call any of this effort, we can simply watch these conflicting parts of ourself and these negative judgements, and trust that we will know what is the next thing to be done. None of this needs to be seen as a snag or an effort. Each personal conflict or negative feeling can be seen as a gift with which we can go deeper into finding out who we are, what the world is, and what we want. I don't say that we must do this in order to be better people; I simply say that to the extent that we *do* do this we will come out of our blindness and delusion and start to see and understand what is going on.

Faith

Another important feature of a religious person is that she has 'faith'. But the crucial question is, what sort of 'faith'? What do we mean by 'faith'? I found three definitions offered in the dictionary for this word. One of these is "confidence, reliance and trust". These, I have mentioned already, and they seem to be essential qualities if we are to cope in this world without constant insecurity and self-torture. The second definition is "Belief proceeding from reliance on authority" and this, too, seems important and valuable. None of us have the time or skill to be able to check the truth of everything that we are told. We have to accept on trust somebody else's word on a subject quite frequently, which doesn't mean that we imagine that they are infallible. We simply assume that they are probably right, and that it is just not worth bothering to check and examine the matter any further unless some good reason for doing so presents itself. We will be particularly inclined to accept 'the authority' if what he says sounds coherent and fits in with what we already know.

These two particular definitions of faith would appear to present no major problems and I don't wish to spend any more time on them. The third and final definition, on the other hand , is much more dubious in value and is the one that is used most often in the context of discussions about religion. This is "Belief in the truths of Holy Scripture and the teaching of the Church". Thus a person says "I believe in the Holy Scripture because I have 'faith' "; and this turns out to mean, "I believe in the Holy Scripture because .... I believe in the Holy Scripture". In other words people offer 'faith' as their reason for believing something; but when you ask them what they meant by 'faith' this reveals itself to be "belief in something without bothering to have any reasons at all".

Thus it is that a person with this sort of faith might be prepared to agree, that by any criteria of evidence, his belief in, say, the historical Jesus is based on flimsy grounds in the extreme. Were he a judge, biographer, scientist or historian he would accept that the evidence is completely inadequate. But does this deter him from believing in the historical Jesus? Not a bit of it! In the role of historian he might conclude that "we just don't know", but then he says that this doesn't matter because he is also 'a believer', he has 'faith'. The yawning gap left by the lack of evidence is filled by faith, but this turns out to be not a new and different kind of evidence, but a blithe disregard for the fact that the evidence is lacking.

This so-called faith, then, is nothing more than a dogged refusal to face facts, or, to put it another way, it is a refusal to recognise that there aren't any solid facts. I can see nothing desirable in such a faith. It seems to involve a lack of courage, a refusal to see that we are largely ignorant of the world and our place in it. It seems to involve an infantile wish for final answers, all-embracing explanations and clear and authoritative instructions about what to do. It is the very essence of an immature personality.

Such faith, such blind belief which simply disregards the

(lack of) evidence, is in fact a form of idolatory. The early Christians were warned not to worship wooden idols, but, instead, Christians have often made idols out of a set of abstractions, or concepts, contained in an old book. It is easy to see idolatory when it involves the worship of material images; but the stubborn clinging to concepts and ideas, however abstract, is also idolatory. Christ himself perhaps, realised this. It is claimed that he said, "You search the scriptures daily, for in them you *think* you have life".

Faith, when understood as absolute certainty about the truth of Scripture or the teachings of (any) Church is, I suggest, worthless. It involves a pretense that belief can be supported even when evidence of any sort is lacking. A person *wants* to believe something, say the detailed stories about Christ or Buddha or Mohammed, and because the evidence doesn't support the belief he pretends that it can be supported by 'faith'.

The interesting thing about this particular definition of faith is that it is the complete opposite of faith when defined as 'confidence, reliance and trust'. When you have confidence you don't need to cling to beliefs that are not supported by evidence. To cling to beliefs in this way in fact shows a fundamental lack of confidence, a lack of faith. It amounts to saying, "Unless these things are true, I cannot face life. Nothing makes sense to me". If we have genuine faith we will have the trust and courage to face and accept life as it is, which includes acknowledging all the unpalatable parts and accepting the fact that we are largely ignorant of many things. Faith, in its genuinely valuable sense, involves remaining open and open-minded. It involves admitting the extent to which we don't know and don't understand. It is not all about pretending that we have a neat set of answers, values and instructions, when the truth is that we haven't.

Faith, then, defined as belief in the truth of Scriptures and the Church is in fact quite contrary to faith in the sense of having confidence, reliance and trust. This latter sort of faith has got nothing to do with belief, really, except that with it you no longer need neurotically to cling to any particular beliefs at all. Beliefs, ideas and concepts can best be regarded as 'maps' that can help us find our way around the world. You can believe in a map in the sense that you are prepared to try it out and make use of it for as long as it seems to be working. But as soon as you start to think "this is one of *my* beliefs, one of *my* maps" you are in great danger of becoming neurotically attached to the map, so that you end up clinging to it even when you find yourself in territory where it is useless.

The person with real confidence and reliance will not make idols out of any maps or ideas, but will merely use them for as long as they seem to be useful. The person with real faith retains an open mind and is prepared to look for new maps when the old ones are no longer working. On the other hand, the person without real faith will say, "I must hang on to these maps come what may. They must be true. I want and need them to be true." Hence the Anglo-Saxon root *lief* which I am told, means to wish. Our present use of the word belief does often fit in with this Anglo-Saxon derivation of the word. Beliefs are not just things that we try out and test to see if they are true; we also *wish* that they were true. The person with real faith, on the other hand, does not have such a strong wish. He or she is prepared to accept the truth as it is, whatever it may be, and regardless of whether or not it fits in with her preconceptions and (be)liefs.

Thus it is, I think, that the scientist, at her best, has great faith, and, indeed, has more faith than the dogmatic theologian. She has beliefs, of course, in the sense that she goes into every situation with ideas and preconceptions that she wishes to test. But she doesn't subbornly cling onto them when the evidence is pointing in another direction. She uses her beliefs for as long as they seem to work, but is quite prepared to search for new ones if this seems necessary. She remains open to the world as it is, and has the faith (confidence and trust) that she will cope with it somehow. This attitude of faith is the very opposite of clinging and holding on. The person who refuses to remain open, who insists that certain propositions about God and the Universe must be true, is a person who has no faith at all. He is clinging on to old maps and mistaking them for reality. He is holding on tight. He is not relaxed with the world as it is. At bottom he is afraid to let go into the world, and so he remains rigid and closed.

God is often seen as protector, father, a firm base in a

changing world. There are many hymns that sing the praises of God as though He was a mighty fortress. Such hymns are not hymns of faith. The person with faith doesn't need a fortress because he is not on the defensive. He doesn't see the world as attacking him. A person with faith tends to see the world as having a fluid , mobile, changing quality rather than being a provider of firm and solid bases. The faithful person doesn't need a fixed base; rather, he is prepared to swim with change and not to cling to the edge of life. The fundamental attitude of faith is that of not clinging on, neither to beliefs not to anything else. It is, rather, an attitude of letting go and trusting in change. And so, for example, the Buddhist word *Nirvana* does not denote a place after life or in life where all is fixed, constant and 'as you think it ought to be'. It means simply, 'to breathe out'. (Or, rather, this is the most valuable definition of Nirvana that I have come across). With faith you let yourself breathe out in this world as it actually is. You trust that the next breath will come, and you trust that you will cope without ever achieving a final definitive map.

Those with real faith know that they don't know, but still have the courage to make commitments. They are 'half sure' but 'whole hearted'! They don't try to clutch at or grasp anything in life with intellect. Intellect is used to provide maps of the world, but they don't confuse the map with reality, and they don't cling to any map.

Thus the person who has genuine faith in God is the person who has faith in the unknown. 'God' ultimately is a label for the Great Unknown, as many a mystic has said. It is a label to denote our ignorance, our sense of the mystery of life rather than an all-embracing explanatory concept. The trouble is, though, that when we label it is easy to pretend that we know what we are talking about, and so I think it is wisest to discard the word altogether.

Immortality

Religion at its heart, I have suggested, is about the way we experience the world and behave in it. It is not realistic, surely, to expect religion or anything else to provide final answers to the fundamental questions about life, and so, to repeat, belief does not lie at the heart of religion.

People who lack faith in the unknown will not be happy with this, and one of the biggest questions that those without faith want answered is the question: "What happens after we die?" Virtually every major and minor religious tradition has attempted to provide answers to this question, and so we have doctrines of immortal souls, Heaven, Hell, reincarnation and much more. It really is quite extraordinary to see how reluctant we are to admit that we simply *don't know* the answers to many questions. Ask most priests of whatever persuasion to tell you what happens after you die and they will generally struggle to find you an answer, although they will often hedge their comments with all manner of qualifications, pointing out that it is "difficult to find words for these matters" and so on. A more direct, simple and honest answer, surely, is "I don't know", and we would be of more service to ourselves and each other if we were more readily to admit this.

If we have faith, we will have strong beliefs and ideas about the world only insofar as there is evidence to support them. And the evidence we have about what happens to us after we have died is not adequate to support any of the grandiose theories and strong beliefs that many people cling on to. What evidence we do have makes it clear that, when a body dies, it rots away and all the behaviours and experiences connected with it disappear as well. This would seem to be just as well. No new life would be possible on this crowded planet unless the older personalities, bodies, ways of behaving and experiencing moved out of the way. Death we tend to see as a great insult and a great snag to life. And yet no new life would be possible without death.

It is very commonly felt that death and life are polar opposites. Life, we imagine, is in conflict with death. Death claims us in the end; we fight a battle that in the end we lose. The spiritual attitude, I would suggest, does not see life and death as being in conflict with each other. Life and death are each simply aspects of the same process of change and movement. Death is inevitable. It is just about the only event that we can predict will happen with any certainty, even though we won't be present to witness it.

When we remember the fact of our mortality, life can have a fizz and excitement in it. When we forget that we will die (as we usually do), life often becomes rather deathly, endless and unfulfilling. Of course there will be times when, on thinking about death, we will feel very scared and alone. But the way to deal with this is to go through this experience, explore it, learn about it, and in this way we can, slowly, move on to other moods and ways of passing the time. It does us no good whatsoever to repress our fears, pretend that we don't feel fear, or invent nursery tale stories about life after death. If we have courage we can face the fact that we feel fear, face the fact that we are moving towards an 'unknown', and in the process we will feel far more alive, and feel more awe and wonder with the mystery of life than will happen if we dull our sensibilities with fantasies and pretences to knowledge.

The strange truth is that the more people refuse to let things die, the more deathly their lives become. For example, a person has a wonderful day with some friends; she has felt really alive and fulfilled and has enjoyed every moment. Eventually, though, the sun comes down on that day. It is over, night comes and a new day must begin. What is she to do? If she tries to cling on to the day that has now gone she will spend all her time living in fantasy. She will spend the next day, and all the days that follow, in fruitlessly trying to re-capture the past. Her attention will be focused on images created in her mind, and these images themselves are likely to fade as the months and years go by. And what will have happened to her awareness of the actual day that she is living in? It will be very dull and lifeless, as I have explored in the chapter on "Awareness". In other words, by seeking to make one particular day, or various aspects of the past, immortal she will have killed the life, energy and awareness in the actual present moment. And remember, there is only one time and place where we can actually *live* our life – HERE and NOW. And if, here and now, all we ever do is live in fantasy and memory, we will have made our life a very deathly and unfulfilling business.

This business of giving up on the present is really very common. Perhaps most people, as they get older, take more and more of their attention away from what is happening

within and around them in their lives and spend most of
their time floating around in a hazy mist of memory.
Obviously there is no harm in this up to a point. We can all
enjoy reminiscences and these can help us get a clearer
understanding of ourselves and our lives. But at some stage
our focus on the past becomes so great that we, as it were,
'kill' the present. Hence the paradox. On the one hand we
fear death and cling to life. On the other, in the very process
of clinging on to old memories we kill off new experience in
our lives long before the moment of physical death. We
worry about the moment of physical death; the truth is that
many people kill themselves psychologically long before
their allotted span of years. Hence the Indian teacher,
Krishnamurti who when asked "What is your opinion of
people committing suicide?" answered, "As far as I can see,
most people have already committed suicide."

Much of our fear of death is the result of our having a false
conception of our 'self' (as I have explored in Chapter Six).
We see ourselves as 'that which we have'; and, with the
prospect of death, we sense that all these things will be lost.
Thus the ancient Egyptian Pharaohs' pathetic attempts to
avoid this loss by cramming their pyramid burial chambers
with as much as possible of their accumulated junk. With a
more spiritual sense of self, death does not lead to 'loss'
because we realise that we never had all these accumulations
in the first place. The whole process of developing an idea of
self as 'that which I have accumulated' leads on to the fear
of death. If we wake up sufficiently to awareness of life we
see that this idea of Self is, after all, just an idea. Thus, to
quote Krishnamurti once again,

"The 'me' is a symbol, not an actuality. Having created the
symbol of the 'me', thought identifies itself with its conclusion, with the formula, and then defends it: all misery
and sorrow come from this."

Most people would agree that "you can't take it with you",
and so few are so foolish as to cram their coffins with
consumer goods. But there is still the hope that 'something'
survives the 'crash' of death, and so there is still the fond
hope in many people's minds that there is a non-physical
'soul' that lives on. This is seen as some sort of non-material
'black box', rather like the flight recorder in the tail of an air-

liner. What is the nature of this soul? people ask, and many clergy valiantly try to answer.

Why don't we just admit that we don't know the answer? I have never come across a non-physical person and I can't even imagine what it would mean to do so. Neither have I met a reincarnated person, and I have no memories of previous lives that I might have lived.* And yet there is an important sense, I think, in which we do all live on after our deaths, which does not require us to indulge in flights of fancy. In this sense, everything we do lives on. Let us look at some examples of this. You smiled at someone at the bus-stop this morning, let us suppose. A brief message of support for, interest in, and contact with, another person. In one important respect that smile can never die because the person who received it will never totally forget it. It will, in some small way, have an influence on what she does with her life.

Someone, maybe twenty years ago, was warm and helpful towards you. Even though you may have forgotten this and were not perhaps conscious of it for long, that help is likely to have made a difference to the way you went about your own life. In this way the good that we do to others can radiate outwards endlessly as it is passed on from one person to another.

If some ancient Greek smiled at some other ancient Greek two or three thousand years ago, then that smile is in an important respect not lost to us. It has passed on and on through the generations, and is part of the stock of memories and attitudes that we now have available to us. Similarly, all the evil, selfishness and competitiveness has been passed on and on. It influences, often for the worse, the behaviour of each new generation. Thus we have vicious cycles of influence that have lasted for thousands of years as well as virtuous ones. All the good and all the harm that we ever

---

*A handful of people do claim to have had such extraordinary experiences, and philosophers have written volumes in an attempt to suggest how we should deal with this. In brief, let me suggest that it is wise in principle to proceed with scepticism and caution, and look first at the most plausible and ordinary explanation available, rather than the most fantastic and revolutionary.

achieve will live on through others, because we are influencing others with everything that we do, all day long. On Tuesday I cheat and lie to someone; that cheating and lying is stored up in some way by that person, and will have its influence, which is not to say that we can predict the outcome. On Wednesday someone enjoys trying to humiliate me. That action, too, will have some impossible to predict consequence.

And so it is for all of us, every day and all day. The very way we carry ourselves though the day, or the extent that we hide away from others, provides a model which others will use either as a source of inspiration or as a burden. We do make a difference. If we have been scowling our way through the days for dozens of years, and looking fearful, aggressive, cold and competitive; then those influences will now already have passed outwards through thousands and thousands of people. If we have listened to others, given them support, as well as showing regard and respect for ourselves, then that too has had an influence. Everything we do and are is a contribution to others, and it is salutory to ask ourselves how far what we have contributed has been a source of inspiration for others and how far it has been a burden that others have had to struggle against.

It goes without saying that it is soon very difficult to trace and measure the contributions we have made, but it is irresponsible to pretend that, because it is hard to detect the difference we make, we therefore don't make any difference. Only those very close to us are likely to be in a position to be able to put labels on our influence and say "this is John's work"; and even the most famous are usually forgotten by everyone after one hundred years. But why this fetish about remembering names? The fact of the influence remains and gets passed on by succeeding generations.

This would seem to be no trivial matter. Everyone alive now is in some way carrying the stock of memories and moods from the past. Whether we let the future fall under the dominance of hatred, greed, and destruction instead of love, generosity and creativity is in the hands of each and all of us.

None of us are mere cyphers, and each of us has choices and options. We are all responsible. But it is also true that we have all been influenced by those who came before us and we all influence those who follow. And in this significant respect we are, I suggest, immortal.

Chapter Eight. Psychology and Religion

Summary

General view that religion provides facts and answers. But question of evidence; poor evidence for the historical Jesus and Buddha. The value in ancient teachings to be found in their suggestions about how to live. But we have to decide for ourselves. Therapists considering the question of what it means to be living to one's full potential were led on to examine religion. We already know much about wisdom; hence our recognition of the great. The wise person doesn't have all the answers. Ritual and belief as pointers to something beyond themselves. Belief not as important as experience and behaviour. 'Being at one with the world'. 'Separation' needed for mind to comprehend the world. Unity can be sensed but not understood intellectually. Strength comes from feeling the support of the world; not from feeling in defiance and at odds with it. 'Things' arising from 'no-thing'. Letting life live though us. Use of the word God? Myth of God and the Devil; various interpretations. Enlightenment. Searching for the miraculous. Teaching by example ... Sufi Master or imposter? Effort, obstacles and conflict. Faith. Immortality. Death. Dying to every moment past.

Questions and Exercises

1. When you feel you need some good advice, form in your mind a really clear picture of a 'wise old person', and then ask him/her to advise you. You will probably get some really valuable suggestions! This mental device is a way of getting you to make use of your own best judgement. This 'wise person', (you), is not infallible, but he/she is wiser than you think. (And, anyway, she's all you've got!)

2. Do you know the experience of being a big successful person, beating others and whipping circumstances into shape? Also, do you know the experience of being small; or being mown-down by others; flattened by circumstances and pushed around by everything?

Now see if both of these experiences can be abandoned. See if you can experience dancing, flowing and co-operating with other people and circumstances, regardless of whatever it is you are doing. A sense of the 'flow' of life can be realised if you just pay attention: thoughts arise and pass away. The breath comes in and goes out again. Actions take place, beginning and ending. Who 'you' are in all of this is a great mystery; and it is possible to experience 'your' thoughts, feelings and actions as though they were like the sounds of a violin in an orchestra. The rest of the orchestra, needless to say, is everything else that is happening all around you.

3. The cat gets on with being a cat; it cannot be out of harmony with everything around it. Whatever it does, it is 'natural'. Trees get on with being trees. Whatever they do, is what trees do. Earth gets on with being earth, water gets on with being water. None of these things are finally separable from any of the others. Humans get on with being humans. They are not more separate and artificial and at odds with things than a bird's nest is at odds with the tree. Everything happens – naturally. See if you can let this truth sink in deep. Watch the way that everything is happening— 'Just like that!' Like what? Like whatever way it *is* happening.

4. Everything is happening in just the way that it happens. Notice that there is nothing that you have to do about this. There is nothing that you *can* do *about* it because you are not separate and seated at some control panel that controls the show. What can a wave do *about* the river, when it is a part of what the river is doing? Similarly, you are part of the whole of life. You can do nothing *about* things, you can only be another one of the things that are happening. And whatever you do, it will always be 'natural'. Naturally you will have plans, preferences and judgements. These are not separate from and 'looking down upon' the movement of life; they are part of this movement.

5. When you have understood all this, you will not have reached anywhere special, or become anything special. You will simply have realised that you and everything else already is amazing, mysterious and miraculous beyond all judgement. You are already special. It is already special for you to have your particular fears, foolishness, plans, feelings and schemes. Consequently, you can be 'at home' and 'at peace' and in the 'right place' right now. Unconditionally. Regardless of wherever that place may be. Without having to lift a finger or change anything about yourself. This will not mean that you become smug and inert. Because a part of who you are right now is that you have got all these plans, ideals, feelings and so on.

6. It really is very strange to try to create exercises to help us achieve spiritual awareness. If we just looked, we could see that everything is already taking care of itself. Our attempting to change things is also taking care of itself. When you know that you have already 'arrived', you will find it much easier to get on to the next place.

7. You can never push a ball out of balance. You can never topple it because, if the force acting on it is strong enough, it will be quite happy to go where it is pushed. Have you got the grace to 'roll with' what cannot be changed? And the courage to change what can be changed? And the wisdom to know the difference? The answer, often, will be "NO". So what are you going to do; sulk about it? If you do it will be quite natural. But sulking won't achieve anything.

8. See if you can have an *effortless* week! When you start to see something as 'effort', see it instead as 'that which is involved in doing what I want to do'. This doesn't mean that you will always be impassive; see the swearing, misery, conflict too as 'that which is involved'. And then you will find that there is a quiet place underneath all the storm and fury. And thus you may find that the week has been effortless. I have known some people who managed this in the first week that they tried it. (And some who didn't!) If you don't manage, tough luck. Forgive yourself. Look at it again.

9. Similarly with 'obstacles' and 'conflict'. See them simply as 'that which is involved ...'. You may find that you can

have a life free of effort, obstacles and conflict. Of course, this doesn't mean that you will avoid all your feelings and always be calm and impassive. You will probably become aware of many more feelings – highs and lows that you had been repressing. However, you simply do not have to see these as effort, obstacles or conflict. Whether or not you do so is in your hands.

10. Invent a ceremony for yourself. Have a special arch and pass though it. Pour $£200 down the nearest drain. Recite some special words. Send me some money! At the end of the ceremony say to yourself: "Now I have really arrived. I no longer need to get to the right place and be the right person in order to live my life. This *is* the right place and I *am* the right person. I shall start here!"

9. Practical Skills and Spiritual Values

What I hope I have managed to do in this book is show that it is impossible, really, to consider the practical skills needed for self-awareness and relationship with others without also looking at the underlying spiritual values that are involved in this. Books that simply try to examine practical skills in day-to-day living without attending to the spiritual aspects are in great danger of nourishing the competitive, fortress, ego. This simply results in people finding new, more sophisticated, ways to manipulate others. On the other hand, books that try to consider spirituality in the abstract, without looking in detail at what this means in terms of day-to-day living tend to encourage a vapid withdrawal from the world.

G. K. Chesterton, I am told, once said that mysticism, " . . . begins in mist, centres on 'I' and ends in schism", and this is a powerful indictment of mysticism at its worst. The common view of the mystic is that he is a person with a long white beard and flowing white robe, who is to be found half-way up a mountain, staring at infinity. His experience, we are to believe, is one of endless bliss. A sort of warm glow constantly bathed in white light. This is all very well, and some people spend a lot of time hanging around mountain-sides or monasteries in order to 'have' such experience. It is seen as the last word in consumer durables; 'White Light and Ecstasy!' . . . reaching the parts that other (material) products fail to reach. Moreover, while trying to achieve such exalted experiences people can develop silly affectations and obsessions about the oriental bric-à-brac or occult gadgetry that, they consider, is required to help them along this path.

Such an attitude gives mysticism or spirituality a bad name. The mystic, monk, or hermit, according to this view, is not 'all here'. If you meet one he will hardly be able to focus his attention on you, because he will be too busy gazing at infinity, or taking in the 'Oneness'. If a small child comes along with shoe laces that have come undone, the mystic will be of no use at all. The child can trip up and hurt herself, and still he will be unmoved and unaware. In any case, he will think, why bother with a child's suffering if suffering is a delusion and the child is a mere speck when measured against infinity? All this is, I think, a common view of the nature of mysticism or spirituality. The mystical experience is seen as 'nice work if you can get it', but is ultimately looked upon as a selfish business as far as getting anything done or relating with others is concerned. The mystic glimpses 'One-ness', but if you want the roof repaired, or a meal this evening, or the child's shoelaces fastened then you need to turn to that poor peasant; the ordinary layperson.

I have sketched what I think is a common view of spirituality or mysticism, but all this is, I think, a very degenerate form of spirituality. (Which is not to say that it is uncommon!) I have no use for the so-called mystic who is not 'all here', as it were, and whose experience is simply a 'golden fugginess'. The only kind of spirituality that I find important is that which makes us more effective in everyday life – both for ourselves and for others. In my view, the spiritual person sees everyday life in its proper context, but this does not involve withdrawing from the everyday world. The spiritual person lives 'in Eternity' if you like; but Eternity is not some fabulous place found in the "Arabian Nights", far away from here and now. Eternity *is*: Right Here, Right Now. When you are here, now, your fears of the future and regrets about the past can diminish and be seen in perspective. And, because you are not carried away with thoughts of past and future you do not sense yourself as being pushed around by time. The sense of time arises merely from that memory or plan that is floating by here and now. Without those thoughts there would be no sense of time and there would not even be a sense of 'now' because this concept only exists in relation to thoughts of past and future.

The mystic, then, is outside of a sense of time because he puts so much more of his energy and attention in the only place it can be effective; which is right here and right now. He is not, in other words, some airy, fairy figure who lacks any solidity and who ignores what is going on. Rather, it is the mystic who is much more solid, much more here and much more aware than the rest of us. It is we who are off in our dreams and avoiding reality. The mystic doesn't gaze endlessly at infinity; he is the one who, on a grey day by the gasworks near the dole queue, will be fully awake to all of this going on around him. Moreover he will tend to want to do something about it and will be likely to be effective in what he does. The mystic will use whatever power he has to the full, but he will not pretend to be omnipotent. In other words, spirituality is not some leisure time activity that can be pleasant or important if you have a spare moment. It is more like an underlying attitude that affects everything you do, and improves your effectiveness in everything you do. Spirituality is not something that happens 9.30–10.00 p.m. after work, washing up or a public meeting; it is rather, the *way* in which you go about these other things.

In search of wise men (*or: "I used to be conceited – but now I'm absolutely perfect!"*)

Feminist readers will understandably stiffen at my use of 'men' rather than 'people'. But I am going to consider delusions under this heading, and one of the big delusions is that the sage or guru is necessarily a man. Critics of the spirituality or enlightenment business will focus on the vapid withdrawal that I have described above and, understandably, will see nothing of value in any of this. Disciples, on the other hand, tend to make all kinds of other mistakes: for example, when we are frightened, insecure and uncertain, it is very tempting to imagine that somewhere in the world there is someone who has all the answers, who can tell us exactly what to do, who really is beyond the everyday ruck of human folly and error. "If only I could find such a master", the would-be disciple thinks, "I would be saved. I would be alright at last."

If you take virtually any human being and surround him with thousands of people who are all convinced that he has

a Hot Line to the Truth, and has finally gone beyond all
human weakness and folly, then you will probably find that
he ends up in believing this himself. It is, I think, the utmost
nonsense. We have all come across people who are wise
beyond the norm, who have many penetrating things to say
about life and living, and who we would do well to listen to.
But I have never met anyone who is 'whiter-than-white', as
it were: who doesn't sometimes come out with remarks and
observations that seem stupid, self-centred, ill thought-out,
childish or whatever. And I never expect to meet such a
person, because I cannot conceive how such a person could
exist. The very idea of such so-called 'perfection' seems full
of contradictions. For example, such a perfect person would
be a bore and therefore not perfect.

All too often, though, the 'Guru-Business' throws up
people who claim to have all the answers, and who expect
others to prostrate themselves at their feet and take in quite
uncritically everything that they say. The motto becomes, 'I
obey, Oh Master, I left my brain at the door!' This is an act
of ultimate folly. The buck stops with each of us. We each of
us have the last word. The 'Great One' can come in on a very
high pedestal, surrounded by uncritical admirers, with a
very tall hat. But I will decide for myself whether what is said
is of any value. I will accept and reject as I see fit. I will use
my own best judgement because, fallible though it is, it is all
I've got. Some people will have a good track record in my
opinion. What they have said will frequently have seemed
valuable and so I will come to expect that what they say next
will be likely to be useful too. But I will not take this for
granted. I will always be on the look-out for error and
foolishness and I will expect to find it occasionally. Surely,
all of us can and should do the same. And so I hope, for example, that you will be better than I have been in throwing
out some of the rubbish that is, no doubt, to be found in this
book. I've done my best to get rid of what I have, on second
thoughts, thought to be inadequate, but others will no doubt
find more to reject.

The genuinely mature person does not pretend to have all
the answers and, paradoxically, is not obsessed with seeking
perfection or avoiding all error. Real wisdom involves finding a balance between, on the one hand, inertia and idle

complacency, and on the other an obsessive wish to do everything right and to get yourself and everything else exactly as you think they 'should' be. Thus, I think, the most useful way of thinking about the wise person is to see him or her as the 'sage-cum-fool'. Anyone who thinks that he has really made it to some ultimate pinnacle of wisdom really is a fool. Greater wisdom is the be found in the person who knows that he is also a fool; who knows that he makes mistakes and is bound to go on doing so, and who has a genuine sense of humour about his own sense of self-importance. The wise person takes himself seriously but not too seriously.

Looking for the "Bed of Roses"

Many people realise that life is not all about arriving at some final place of 'perfection'. They accept that neither they, nor others, nor the world as a whole, will ever fit anybody's ideals. But many, even though they accept that there is no final destination, want the journey itself to be a primrose path, as it were. They want, when deciding what is to be done next, to always be able to find a bed-of-roses option. An option that will not involve large doses of pain, confusion, set-backs, doubt, despair, hatred, fear and all the other thorns of life. The truth, of course, is that quite often there is not a hassle-free option available. The pains are part of life just as much as the pleasures, in the way that valleys are an integral part of hill-tops! The irony is there to be seen even in the image of a bed of roses. After all, a natural bed of roses would also be full of thorns!

Suffering, pain, set-backs and all the rest are not delusions. They are real enough! Much suffering and pain comes from trying to resist pain when it is unavoidable. But, even when you accept it, it may not go away! That is why going with pain and learning from it requires courage; little real bravery would be needed if all these things were in some sense illusory. Of course we will seek to avoid pain and suffering, but it is impossible to avoid it all the time, just as it is impossible to travel on a journey and always be on mountain peaks.

This is a real difficulty for therapists, or spiritual teachers or almost anyone in a helping role. People, so often, want to be saved from facing discomfort and unhappiness and all the other darker sides of life. When the pain comes from self-defeating behaviour then much can be done to reduce it. But not all pain comes from this, And then the helper, if she is really to help, must encourage the person to face her unhappiness, or confusions, or whatever and try to learn from it; try to see what it is telling her about herself and her life.

This is often the last thing that people want. Rather they want a free lunch. They want a way out that involves no risks or challenges, a solution that others can hand out on a plate and that is entirely comfortable. It may well be that we are right to keep some painful facts about ourselves and others at a distance. Perhaps we are right to keep some parts of the unconscious unconscious. If we opened ourselves up too quickly to everything we had hidden away and swept under the carpet then we might not be able to cope very well. Similarly, we are no doubt right to use tranquillisers sometimes to deal with physical pain. It is, always, a question of balance. But the search for painless solutions, and short-term comforts at the expense of long-term well-being, seems at present to be quite excessive and not in our best interests. A masochistic search for pain would be pointless and silly, but we in the West seem to go to the other extreme in our preference for drugs and dishonesty.

Confronting those aspects of ourselves and our lives that are painful is not at all easy. It works best, needless to say, when we are getting a lot of support from others and when we feel basically supportive of ourselves. I can face my darker self to the extent that I unconditionally support, love and accept myself; and others, similarly, can help me do this when they too have an underlying positive attitude towards me. What none of us are prepared to put up with, (unless we are masochists), is a demand that we confront our 'nasty' features from people who feel hostile towards us.

When someone is hostile, judgemental and aggressive towards me then I will resist facing up to what he tells me regardless of how correct his criticisms may be. I will resist him all the way. I will resent his attack and I will, rightly, imagine myself to be defending my integrity. And so it is that aggressive attempts to change others always creates resistance. Whereas acceptances of weaknesses and failings, in a warm and supportive way, without judgement or condescension, is much more likely to result in changes.

Britishness and the 'stiff upper lip'

Popular psychology is big business in the U.S.A., where people are as keen to overhaul their personalities as they are willing to try to 'improve' everything else in their world. I have a great respect for the New World energy and enthusiasm, and belief that things can be changed for the better. Certainly I prefer it to the cynicism and weariness of so much of European culture; but, on the other hand, *some* of the European scepticism about American enthusiasm does seem well founded.

It is fair to say, I think, that many Europeans regard America as naïve and infantile. Americans, it is felt, simply haven't yet discovered the limits of the possible. They still think that they have limitless frontiers and that anything can be done. This is, of course, an enormous generalisation to make about 250 million people, but there is, I think, a grain or more of truth in it. Certainly such an attitude is clearly to be seen in many popular U.S. best sellers in psychology. Again and again, the willing reader will be promised that whatever he can clearly imagine can be turned into reality. If only we become responsible and use our powers to the full, the charlatans promise, then we can become omnipotent. Think out clearly you wildest dreams; get a clear picture of them in your mind ... and then you can proceed to turn them into reality!

This really is so much nonsense. At its worst, it leads to books that will show how *everyone* can become a millionaire, with the right smile, the right positive attitude, and all the rest of the ballyhoo. Such writers *have* seized upon an important truth, because positive attitudes, 'daring to win', confidence and determination *are* undoubtedly of much greater importance than many of us realise. But it is foolish fantasy and involves delusions of grandeur to imagine that attitudes and personal qualities alone determine and guarantee success in this limited and unjust world. And, in any case, what kind of culture is it that it so fascinated by millionaires?

As limitations and constraints close in on the American culture it seems to get ever more desperate in its resolute wish to believe that all doors can be opened and all difficulties overcome. Religious fundamentalism, million-seller instant solutions and increased arms spending all seem to be aspects of this latent fear of failure and limitation. It is to be hoped that this energetic culture can pass through these traumas without either collapsing into despair or blowing us all up in an orgy of hopeless defiance.

In Britain and Europe the mood is very different. We do not think that everyone can be a millionaire, and, in psychology, there is a tendency to think that little, if any, real personal change is possible. I think that these differences can be detected among professional psychologists. Americans tend to be much more optimistic about what people can achieve whereas Europeans focus more on how deeply ingrained old habits can be, and how difficult it is to change any of them. Existentialism in Europe is all about going with despair, anxiety, fear, doubt, insecurity and the awful difficulty of courageous action. American existentialism, on the other hand, looks much more at human potential, joy, ecstasy, sharing and celebration. I want to take a mid-Atlantic position in all of this, without, I hope, leaving myself too much at sea!

The 'stiff upper lip' mentality, then, in my view, is not courageous fortitude in a vale of tears; too often, rather, it is all about repressing one's feelings to no useful purpose whatever. It is weakness rather than strength, and it involves the pretense that any display of one's feelings is an indulgence. It may well be that some people do indulge their feelings and become self-obsessed in their interest in psychology. But when this happens they do not really benefit from what psychology has to offer. You find yourself by going beyond yourself, and so if you use psychology simply as a mirror with which to stare at yourself you learn very little indeed. The test of how far you have learned anything about human relationships and personal awareness lies in what you actually *do* with this information, and this involves far more than, as it were, staring at yourself in a mirror. It involves getting out and relating with other people, finding your strengths and interests, and acting on them.

It is extraordinary really that, as a result of the 'stiff upper lip' mentality, the British put so little time and energy into looking at their own lives and relationships with others. People will go to great lengths to get in the groceries, get promotion at work or re-decorate the house; but they will just assume that their relationships with others and their own mental and spiritual well-being can be left to take care of themselves without any conscious examination at all. And so it is that we find so many human relationships in such a poor state of decay. We let them 'slop about' all over the place, as it were, and allow ourselves to fall into all sorts of destructive patterns of behaviour. Just a little more thought, attention and care could greatly help to reduce all this, and yet so many people think that to do this is selfish, or self-obsessed or an indulgence.

Keeping relationships, of whatever sort, in good repair is considered to have very low priority indeed, and people think that either there is nothing they can do about these matters or that they can safely be left to take care of themselves. I am not just talking about relationships within the family, of course. I am referring to every possible type of relationship, intimate or not, that goes on between people. The quality of such relationships crucially determines what people living and working together can achieve, regardless of what it is that they are trying to do. And, certainly, this affects their overall well-being. And so psychology is not simply a study of individuals, and it is not all about an individualistic approach to life. The truth is that we are not isolated individuals. We grow and find meaning, not just by being on our own, but also by relating with others and co-operating with them. Psychology, then, is important for anyone interested in trying to understand how any sort of co-operative or collective action is possible.

Self or Society?

This book has considered the question of how far it is possible for people to change and make changes. It assumes that we can 'move' ourselves quite substantially given the determination to do so. But it does not, I hope, imply that change is easy. Some critics of psychology say that it is hopeless to try to make alterations by looking at what individuals do, either on their own or with others. Rather, the critics assert, we must look at the social, political and economic institutions within which people live, and try to make changes here. Change is only possible, some say, if you change the system within which people live; then and only then would it be useful to look at individual patterns of behaviour, and you would find that the individual relationships would have altered automatically as a result of such political, social and economic change. And so it is that we find people on the Left in politics saying, 'Bring about Socialism and the quality of personal life and relationship will improve'; while people on the Right will say that more capitalist enterprise will bring about this improvement in personal and community life.

There is, I think, no doubt that many therapists and others in caring roles tend to focus on individuals and small groups without paying sufficient attention to the social, political and economic context within which their clients live. Often it will be the case that a person not only needs to listen more effectively, be more assertive, more aware or whatever; but also they will be in dire need of better housing accommodation, and a job, and a greater say in their community. It is foolish, though, to suggest that because housing and jobs are important then assertiveness and listening are not, just as it would be silly to say that housing and jobs are irrelevant, and that only assertiveness matters. So often there is this needless polarisation, with some people bothering only about individuals and relationships and ignoring the social context, while others plan for social revolution while ignoring the chaos and confusion of their own personal relationships. It is absurd to imagine that we have to make a choice between the Personal and the Political. The truth is that these are each simply aspects of the one overall process such that each influences the other. There are limits to the degree of personal change that can take place without social change, and social improvement is limited by the quality of personal awareness and human relationship. In other words, you cannot really separate the personal from the political and, in any case, psychology is not simply about the personal because Self can only be found in Community. We can only find out who *we* are in relation to the way we are with others.

This is a point worth reiterating, because so often popular psychology has been seen as an example of self-help in isolation from others; of going it alone and sorting things out for yourself. The truth is that we cannot do everything for ourselves and by ourselves, and you haven't understood the notion of responsibility if you think that it is all about doing everything for yourself and going it alone. To do this shows a lack of trust in others and a refusal to face the extent to which we all depend on and are depended upon by others. The responsible person, is not one who refuses to help people and who turns down help from others. With a real understanding of responsibility, we tend to get much better at co-operating with others; leaning on them and also supporting them, whenever one or the other seems desirable.

Psychology and Morality

This book has had quite a lot to say about morality, but always, and rightly I think, in the context of looking at something else; assertiveness or responsibility or whatever. The subject of morality is fascinating in that it is both tortuously complicated and extremely simple. In its essence, let me suggest, it rests on one great insight; namely, that fulfillment comes when we love ourselves and love others as ourselves. But turning this principle into practice is anything but simple.

It is not that we are *instructed* by some supernatural force or secular power to adopt this principle of living. If you follow it out of fear for the consequences or blind obedience then you have not really grasped it at all. Ultimately, we can only live according to this principle to the extent that we see that we are not separate beings at odds with the rest of the world, but that we are ultimately in harmony with everything else. Such a vision of our interconnectedness is very rare, but the more we have it and develop it the more we discover that we simply don't *want* to trample over others or mould them into our preferred shape. Most of us have sufficient awareness to see that, in our heart of hearts, we don't wish to harm our brothers and sisters – even though we also have aggressive and destructive feelings towards them. But few of us can often sense that everyone is our brother and sister. Nonetheless, other people are, in an important sense, related to us, and it is simple ignorance of this which leads us to exploit them. We ignore our interconnectedness with others and we refuse to face up to the harm that we often do to others. When we face all this we can start to change.

Immorality then, as has so often been suggested over the years, is the result of ignorance and blindness. It arises from the delusion that we are separate beings at odds with and at war with others. The more we sense our interconnectedness with others, the more we realise that as soon as we try to damage others we damage ourselves. We thus begin to realise that it really is to everyone's benefit for us all to try to seek compromises that everyone can accept. This involves having respect both for our needs and wishes and for the needs and wishes of others. It requires a capacity to empathise with others; to reach out and see what the world looks like from someone else's viewpoint.

No neat and easy formula is available for finding compromises that all can accept, and it is often difficult to know if one's own or someone else's integrity is being violated. We each of us have to use our own best judgement in all of this and this judgement is fallible but it is all we've got. There simply isn't a Golden Rule Book or Great Authority that can be the final arbiter in resolving moral issues. And all this is made all the more difficult because each of us has within us so many destructive and manipulative tendencies. Moreover, quite often choices of whatever sort will involve pain and suffering for someone.

Moral action in its essence, then, is extremely simple: "Love oneself and love one another as oneself". But in regard to everyday details it is often extraordinarily difficult.

In a sense, this entire book explores what it means to live by the insight that we need to love others and love ourselves. Nothing that I have said about assertiveness or guilt or worry or relaxation or anything else makes any real sense if it is separated from this one basic insight. Whenever practical skills in psychology are used by someone with a basic attitude of competitiveness and separation, then the results are simply more, and more sophisticated, manipulation and exploitation of others. The competitive person is not aided by these skills but *armed* with them; and he or she goes off and uses them against others. It is well worth noticing that there is not a single good thing under the sun that cannot be (mis)used as a weapon against others! Thus, for example, we can listen to people so that they let down their armour; and then we can smash into them with some cutting remark! Or we can assert ourselves without any empathy for others so that we behave like a steam-roller. Or we can have great awareness of others and then go in ruthlessly at their weak points. Or we can relax and remain quite indifferent to others. Or we can live by very high ideals and show contempt or condescension towards those who don't seem to manage so well. This list could be extended much more and continues to the limits of our creative viciousness. In other words, any of our virtues can be co-opted by most of our vices so that the end result is vicious.

I say this not in order to encourage us to despair, but in order that we face facts. Loving and accepting ourselves and others involves discovering the layer upon layer of competitiveness and destructiveness of which all of us are capable. Seemingly endless forgiveness of ourselves and others would appear to be necessary. A balance has to be found between giving up in despair or inertia on the one hand, and expecting too much of ourselves on the other.

How far from the ideal?

It has not been the purpose of this book to survey what is going on in the society as a whole; in its institutions and among its interest groups, (the book is long enough as it is). I have looked at the various kinds of self-defeating behaviour that are so common among individuals and so, for example, I have explored how far we behave irresponsibly, without awareness, using guilt, lacking love, with needless tension and without honesty. It doesn't take much to see how far all this is reflected in our social, political and economic institutions and among all classes and sections of society. To the extent that the self-defeating behaviour manifests itself on these wider stages we will find that the clergy are dormitory attendants encouraging people to sleep through their lives with a few reassuring rituals and beliefs. The economy will be based on the assumption that all we want to do is to grab as many material things for ourselves as we can regardless of the costs to others. Work, among the self-defeating, will be seen as a great snag to life that demands compensation rather than a means to fulfillment.

The person lacking practical skills and spiritual values lives in the illusion of being separate, and at the level of society as a whole the consequences of such an attitude are obvious: Separations are made between 'us' and 'them'. 'We' are good and right, needless to say, and 'they' are bad and wrong. 'They' may be the Russians, or the Military Establishment, or Trade Unionists or Capitalists. Having sorted out who 'they' are, we then indulge ourselves in orgies of self-righteousness, condescension, aggression, manipulation and all the rest. And who is this person lacking practical skills and spiritual values? Well, all of us to a greater or lesser extent!

To the extent that we wish to defeat ourselves, we will talk about education (Latin: *educere* which means to draw out that which is inside the person) but we will build schools to 'school' people into swimming like porpoises in formation. We talk about the importance of having people think for themselves, but we will try to condition people to unquestioningly accept society's prejudices. We will talk about the importance of having people think and feel for themselves, but we will be scared of feelings which don't 'fit in' and which we can't 'control'. In politics we will give the occasional mention of the importance of statesmanship, but instead we will value manipulation, dishonesty, polarisation, image-making, windy rhetoric and righteousness. We will talk of law and order and pride ourselves on our decency, but we will ignore the violence that the State can and does commit against citizens and foreigners, and we will ignore the violence of our own inhumanity to others.

Finally, for as long as, and to the extent that, we live under the illusion of separation and with self-defeating ways, we talk about peace, brotherhood and goodwill to all people, and then imagine that we must *fight* for peace against all those other bad and wrong people.

To what extent do all these self-defeating ways manifest themselves in society as a whole? That is for each of us to decide and, in part, in depends upon how optimistic or pessimistic we are feeling. But one thing, I think, is certain; that is that we already know what the virtues are and what they involve both in private and in public life. We already know how to live honourably, joyfully and with integrity and we have known for centuries. Usually our practice, though, is far, far away from our ideals. Let us face it: it is true.

What, then, is to be done? Despair or self-flagellation don't do us any good. Expecting to be able to achieve such ideals or get anywhere near them is probably quite unrealistic. Inertia and indifference don't seem adequate. We simply have to face the facts of our destructive behaviour and do our very best to change, with a constant compassion for ourselves and others which doesn't hide from the truth. With luck, we will learn and change and manage to avoid blowing ourselves to pieces.

On the other hand, unless humanity does make some reasonably substantial progress in the morality of its behaviour, then it is very hard to see how further significant development for this species will be possible. We probably won't wipe ourselves out altogether; but we will do too much damage to ourselves and each other to be able to grow up very much further. We will get stuck. We will remain fearful, untrusting, separate from each other, at odds with the world, anxious and unaware.

I don't think that this *has* to be the future of humanity, but it is quite a strong possibility. Most species eventually get stuck at some level of development. Perhaps we have already reached the point where we have stopped growing any more; where further maturity is beyond us. Perhaps, for example, the old saying, "From each according to his ability, to each according to his need", will remain as hopelessly idealistic as it is at present. We are simply not grown up enough to live by such an ideal at the moment, and this is the greatest obstacle to the achievement of any genuinely democratic and humanitarian society.

Whether we do manage to grow up a little more, though, is in our hands. We can start now.

Chapter Nine. Practical Skills and Spiritual Values

Summary

You cannot separate practical skills from spiritual values, if you do you get either ego-trips or withdrawal from the world.

The stereotype of the mystic; and the truth?

Gurus as 'know-alls'

People actually want a know-all when they don't want to take responsibility.

Maturity is not about having all the answers or obsessively seeking 'perfection'.

Ideals cannot be 'reached', You cannot even imagine what this would mean.

The notion of the 'sage-cum-fool'.

'Bed-of-roses' option; often there isn't one.

If you are to confront people you need to support them.

U.S.A. enthusiasm and utopianism. European despair.

The 'stiff upper lip' mentality.

The undervaluing of relationships. Just letting them 'slop' all over the place.

Psychology not just about individuals and individualism; we can only really find ourselves when we look beyond ourselves.

Personal *or* political – a false choice.

Self *or* society – a false choice.

Psychology and morality – in essence simple; in detail complex and difficult.

The whole book based on one moral principle? – Love ourselves and love others as ourselves.

Not because we think we 'should', but because we *see* that this is what works for all of us. When we do anything else we simply suffer; all of us.

Vices can co-opt virtues.

Forgiveness and tolerance but not inertia.

How self-defeating behaviour is reflected in society.

Will we blow ourselves up? Need to be more serious about virtues.

Will we grow anymore? It is in our hands. We can start now.

Questions

1. This is intended to be a practical book. Do you think it will help you to make any practical difference in your life?

YES NO

2. Have you already tried to put some of the ideas and techniques into practice? YES NO

3. If not, do you *intend* to put some of what you have read into practice? YES NO

4. If 'yes' when will you make a serious start? Have you got a good excuse for delaying?

5. Do you think you have made any practical progress with any of these ideas and techniques so far?

YES NO

6. A good way of finding out whether or not you have got anywhere is to ask someone you know whether *they* think you've made any progress toward particular goals you have set. It is not enough to trust simply on your own subjective judgement. For example, it is no good thinking that you have become a better listener if you cannot find a single person who agrees with you about this. Other people's judgements can be distorted too; but you can get a better picture when you start checking around. In, say, six months time will you do this?

7. Remember: If you are really to get anywhere with what this book is all about, it will almost entirely depend on what you do now you have finished reading it. You will need to set yourself goals that are neither too hard nor to easy with lots of 'sub-goals' that you can achieve next week and next month as well as the long-term goals. Obviously, it is entirely up to you, whether you use the material, reject it or forget it.

8. This has been a book about *self*-help therapy. About seeing what, essentially, you can do about yourself with

yourself. However, I don't want to give the impression that you can, or should, always 'go it alone' with all of this. You will probably find that what you have read is more useful, and comes more 'alive', if you can share it with other people. Also, it may be that you are presently facing such severe personal problems that it is quite unrealistic to expect to be able to come to grips with them on your own – with this, or any other, book! In which case, I hope that you will use this book, not as a *substitute* for seeking support from others, but as a means of *helping* you to seek this support.

Suggested Reading

Anderson, M.S. & Savary, L.M. *Passages: A Guide for Pilgrims of the Mind*, Turnstone, 1974

Axline, V. *Dibs: In Search of Self*, Penguin, 1978

Berne, E. *Games People Play*, Penguin, 1970

Bloch, S. *What is Psychotherapy?* Oxford, 1982

Brandon, D. *Zen in the Art of Helping*, Routledge, 1976

Carnegie, D. *How to Stop Worrying and Start Living*, World's Work, 1962

Clare, A. *Let's Talk About Me*, BBC, 1981

Dyer, W. W. *Pulling Your Own Strings, How to Stop Being a Victim*, Hamlyn, 1979

Ernst, S. & Goodison, L. *In Our Own Hands, A Book of Self-Help Therapy*, Women's Press Ltd. 1981

Ferrucci, P. *What We May Be*, Turnstone, 1982

Glasser, W. *Reality Therapy*, Perennial, Harper Row, 1965

Gordon, T. *Parent Effectiveness Training*, Plume, 1975

Kovel, J. *A Complete Guide to Therapy*, Penguin, 1978

LeShan, L. *How to Meditate: A Guide to Self-Discovery*, Turnstone, 1983

Perls, F. et. al. *Gestalt Therapy*, Penguin, 1979

Perls, F. *Gestalt Therapy Verbatim*, Bantam, 1976

Rainwater, J. *You're in Charge: A Guide to becoming your own Therapist*, Turnstone, 1979

Rhinehart, L. *The book of Est*, Abacus, 1977

Rogers, C.R. *A Way of Being*, Houghton Mifflin, 1980

Rowe, D. *Depression, The Way Out of Your Prison*, Routledge, 1983

Satir, V. *Peoplemaking*, Souvenir, 1972

Storr, A. *The Art of Psychotherapy*, Secker & Warburg, 1983

Winn, D. *The Whole Mind Book: An A-Z of Theories, Therapies and Facts*, Fontana, 1980

Watts, A. *The Wisdom of Insecurity*, Rider, 1974